Formerly
New Directions for
Mental Health Services

Gil G. Noam
Editor-in-Chief

NEW DIRECTIONS FOR YOUTH DEVELOPMENT

Theory
Practice
Research

spring | 2002

A Critical View of Youth Mentoring

Jean E. Rhodes | *editor*

JOSSEY-BASS
A Wiley Company
www.josseybass.com

A CRITICAL VIEW OF YOUTH MENTORING
Jean E. Rhodes (ed.)
New Directions for Youth Development, No. 93, Spring 2002
Gil G. Noam, Editor-in-Chief

Microfilm copies of issues and articles are available in 16mm and 35mm, as well as microfiche in 105mm, through University Microfilms Inc., 300 North Zeeb Road, Ann Arbor, Michigan 48106-1346.

ISSN 1533-8916 (print)   ISSN 1537-5781 (online)   ISBN 0-7879-6294-5 (print)

NEW DIRECTIONS FOR YOUTH DEVELOPMENT is part of The Jossey-Bass Psychology Series and is published quarterly by Wiley Subscription Services, Inc., a Wiley company, at Jossey-Bass, 989 Market Street, San Francisco, California 94103-1741. Periodicals postage paid at San Francisco, California, and at additional mailing offices. Postmaster: Send address changes to New Directions for Youth Development, Jossey-Bass, 989 Market Street, San Francisco, California 94103-1741.

SUBSCRIPTIONS cost $70.00 for individuals and $135.00 for institutions, agencies, and libraries. Prices subject to change. Refer to the order form at the back of this issue.

EDITORIAL CORRESPONDENCE should be sent to the Editor-in-Chief, Dr. Gil G. Noam, Harvard Graduate School of Education, Larsen Hall 601, Appian Way, Cambridge, MA 02138 or McLean Hospital, 115 Mill Street, Belmont, MA 02478.

Cover photograph by Getty Images.

Jossey-Bass Web address: www.josseybass.com

Contents

Introduction

THE ADOLESCENT POPULATION in the United States is over twenty million, and internationally it is over five hundred million. We are so accustomed to viewing these statistics with trepidation: to some, they signal violence and drug use, or increased risks of depression and suicide. Right-wing extremists in Europe attack foreigners; youth worldwide serve as soldiers for all kinds of causes. The media have picked up on these risks and report far more frequently on the dramatic dangers of youth than on the positive potential of young people, covering behaviors from bullying to drug dealing to school shootings. Danger, threat, and anxiety sell far better than prosocial behavior.

But the reality of young people's lives is far more complex than the news stories or some of these statistics seem to indicate. The majority of youth are a great resource to our society—they are creative and provide time, energy, and insight into the development of new ideas, community innovation, and volunteerism.

When we think about the lives of our youth, then, the goal is not to choose between recognizing positive youth development or risk. Both perspectives have to go hand-in-hand. But we have far too long viewed adolescence as a time of crisis and danger, and we need to understand the positive and productive aspects of this important time in life.

This journal is dedicated to this shift of thinking. It is unique, created for an amazingly innovative time and an emerging field. New Directions for Youth Development: Theory, Practice, and Research

I would like to thank a number of friends and colleagues who have been extremely helpful in making *New Directions in Youth Development* possible. Their support, intelligence, and passion of the past year will benefit the journal for a long time: Cindy and Ron Hann, Kurt Fischer, Douglas Darling, Donald Lamm, Alan Rinzler, Paul Sidel, and as always Maryanne Wolf. The project first evolved during my stay at the Center for Advanced Study in the Behavioral Sciences in Palo Alto, California.

NEW DIRECTIONS FOR YOUTH DEVELOPMENT, NO. 93, SPRING 2002 © WILEY PERIODICALS, INC.

is committed to youth: their potential, their futures, and their everyday lives. All of us—policymakers, researchers, practitioners, educators, clinicians, and parents—must relearn to build schools that really work for kids, to train a new generation of mental health professionals who learn how to assess not only disorders but also strengths, and to provide training and funding so that the best and brightest practitioners will enter the field and stay in it. Cities have to change to become open places for children and families; out-of-school time has to be organized so that youth learn and have fun while parents work. As we move toward these goals, the challenges we face are huge. But we are in the middle of a transformation! Those dedicated to the healthy growth of youth are creating innovations and inroads, and youth themselves are natural innovators.

What has been missing is a journal that reflects these trends, one that serves as a place of exchange, discussion, and debate, where ideas and research live alongside practical recommendations and policy debates. We also need a journal in which researchers, thinkers, policymakers, and practitioners can come together to forge a strong intellectual underpinning to this emergent field of youth development. There are, of course, excellent books, magazines, and journals dealing with adolescents and positive youth development. We view those who work through those venues as our partners. The field needs all of us to help create a strong foundation. Our focus will be, in the New Directions series tradition, to tackle controversial, interesting, and difficult topics and to devote a whole volume to in-depth discussion of a specific topic, explored from many sides.

We will be provocative and informative, favoring essays that provide research evidence and practical case examples. Taken together, the topics will keep the diverse readership concerned with the well-being of youth, families, and communities involved in an intellectual discourse with practical implications. And as youth culture is becoming almost universal, the scope of the journal will include local, national, and international efforts.

The journal will reflect the creativity of the field. Rather than force issue editors and authors to comply with a set format, we will experiment with many different ways of presenting material. Some volumes will present five or six essays of equal length. Others will have many short position papers. Still others will consist of a few lead papers and many responses. What matters to me as the editor-in-chief is that we address timely issues in a way that fosters dialogue in the field. If a big event occurs, such as that of September 11, 2001, the journal will make room to create a public forum for discussion.

An impressive group of advisers will be guiding me as we produce this journal, providing me with ideas and added expertise. Their fields span psychology, psychiatry, anthropology, community development, adolescent development, education, risk analysis, sociology, and the practice and policy of youth development. But it is not only this board of experts that will serve as consultants. We will also ask you, the readership, to provide us with ideas. I hope that you will let me know of topics that are important in your work, wherever it might be.

This journal serves as a bridge at a time when many fields are converging around a common focus. Everyone contributes to building this bridge and should actively suggest ways in which we can work more closely together: practitioners, researchers, program innovators, funders, librarians, educators, therapists, and policy-makers. The more you can see this journal as your own, the more relevant it will become. Please send me correspondence regarding your reactions to volumes and essays; whenever possible, we will publish your responses either in a future issue or on a Web site dedicated to the journal.

In this first communication with you, I do not want to hide behind the ideas and concepts but give you a sense of what I bring to the task of editor-in-chief and why I decided to take on this job.

My work has been that of a child and adolescent clinician and researcher, trained both in clinical and developmental psychology in Europe and the United States. With a joint appointment between a medical school and an education school, I became interested in adolescent research and childhood problems from a developmental point of view. I also focused on creating prevention programs in schools. What I did not expect was that the work in schools bridging education and mental health would soon lead me to become involved in research and training in after-school time. The work alongside my team clearly indicated that any prevention efforts need to include families and communities and, significantly, after-school time. My developmental thinking shifted increasingly to studying the topic of resilience and finding the strengths in youth to overcome obstacles.

In some ways, I continue to do today what I began two decades ago; my passions are those of the many of us who want to see youth make their best contributions to our society. Youth inherit from us a fragile world. What we thought were peaceful times, ideal when compared to earlier epochs, have shifted. More than ever, we need to make our youth true partners, for they have to take part in solving the significant issues that face our times.

This journal is dedicated to helping this process through providing knowledge, experimentation in practice, and large-scale efforts to change our thinking and our policies. I hope you will join me in making this *our* journal, using it as a forum to inspire and inform all of us who are shaping the lives of young people.

Gil G. Noam
Editor-in-Chief

Editors' Notes

MENTORING HAS BECOME an extremely important, even essential, aspect of youth program planning. What was once reserved for disadvantaged youth is now seen as an almost necessary inoculation for all youth. Advocacy organizations, such as the National Mentoring Partnership, have helped to spur the rapid expansion of programs, and politicians routinely mention mentoring in their speeches. Mentoring has even come to represent a form of patriotism, as exemplified by President George W. Bush's recent decree that those of us in the United States could help win the war against terrorism through volunteerism at home, by tutoring or mentoring a child. General Colin Powell is well known for heading America's Promise, a national mentoring organization that has brought major recognition and legitimacy to the field.

Implicit in these continuous calls for the expansion of mentoring are strong assumptions regarding its benefits. But just how effective are youth mentoring and other programs that foster positive relationships between young people and adults? The answer to this question is complicated by imprecision over what exactly constitutes meaningful mentoring. The familiar one-to-one, volunteer, community-based mentoring is increasingly sharing the stage with many other forms of mentoring: school-based, workplace, group, peer, and even e-mail mentoring. Although the recent literature contains a growing number of studies of conventional mentoring programs, researchers have barely turned their interest toward these newer variations.

A new and exciting application of mentoring is during out-of-school time. After-school programs serve ever larger numbers of children across the United States and provide institutional yet flexible settings where adults are encouraged to mentor youth. With increasing federal, state, and local funds being used for after-school

NEW DIRECTIONS FOR YOUTH DEVELOPMENT, NO. 93, SPRING 2002 © WILEY PERIODICALS, INC.

time, evaluations are being conducted to trace the successes and challenges of current programming. Mentoring will likely become part of these evaluation efforts, making imperative a discussion about what constitutes productive and supportive relationships between adults and youth. Although many practitioners are involved in setting up mentoring programs, only a small group of people dedicate scholarly work to this field, which is increasingly in need of feedback. People in the field tend to see mentoring as a foregone conclusion, something most children and programs should have. After all, who can argue with the need for support, encouragement, consistency, and a one-on-one experience outside the home?

Yet many serious questions and concerns remain. What are the rates of either adults or youths dropping out of mentoring programs and for what reasons? Is it possible that, despite all good intentions, these relationships will actually harm some youth? What are the long-term effects of these broken relationships? What is the need for good training and consultation, given that many mentored youth are at high risk, with difficult family, school, and community relationships? What settings support meaningful mentoring, and what factors hinder the development of productive relationships? How do productive mentoring relationships typically develop, and what makes them so productive, as compared to the dyads that seem to be less effective? We cannot answer all of these questions in this volume, but we can begin the explorations that should continue over time. A first step is to take a realistic and critical view of mentoring so that we can make this field as strong as it deserves to be.

In addition to evaluating the many new forms of mentoring, a key role for scholars will be to raise challenging questions and thoughtful critiques of the mentoring movement. Unsubstantiated claims about mentoring's effectiveness have lent a patina of superficiality to the field that might have discouraged psychologists, educators, and sociologists from pursuing serious studies. And when researchers do persevere to undertake complex analyses, the mentality of presenting the wider culture with only good news about mentoring tends to undermine the impact of any legitimate empirical findings they might report.

Against this background—the practical significance of mentoring and the lack of evidence from the research world—we decided to publish this early volume of *New Directions for Youth Development* on this topic. It is because of these trends that we call this volume *A Critical View of Youth Mentoring*. We mean by this not that we are critical of mentoring or of the many people who have dedicated important personal and societal resources to mentoring youth. Rather, we agreed to focus on research and innovative programming to generate a broad discussion. We wanted to assure a nonideological exploration of the conditions that support mentoring and those that can actually have negative effects. We also decided to focus on new applications of mentoring and, in line with the goals of the journal, to address theory, practice, and research issues.

This volume provides evidence of the benefits of enduring mentoring programs of high quality. In addition, apprenticeships, advisories, and other relationship-based programs show considerable promise. More generally, researchers working in a broad array of disciplines have highlighted the protective benefits of caring adults in the lives of youths. Additional research is needed to identify both the contexts in which caring relationships are most likely to arise and the range of protective relationships within those contexts. Of course, the ultimate goal in identifying protective factors that help young people thrive in difficult environments is to understand not only *what* but *why* and *how*. In answering the latter questions, most scholarship, including the research on mentoring, has come up short. Previous work has not adequately explained how mentoring promotes change and why some adolescents benefit from the support more than others. Practitioners need a deeper understanding of the developmental processes that govern nonparent adult relationships, such as the ways in which they operate within, and depart from, the emotional frameworks developed through parent-child relationships. We should also explore adults' motivations for engaging in relationships with unrelated adolescents, the effects of these motivations on commitment to the relationship, and, importantly, the influence of these relationships on mentors. Examining methods that move beyond the individual mentor or protégé to capture the larger context in which relationships unfold will enrich our understanding of such issues.

Scholarly attention to the processes that govern nonparent adult relationships, and the contexts that give rise to them, could shed additional light on this important topic. As mentoring continues to expand, it is imperative that researchers converge on a theoretically informed and practically applicable understanding of youth-adult relationships. *A Critical View of Youth Mentoring* was written with just such a goal in mind. The chapters in this volume are likely to enhance the conversation around relationship-based interventions and generate new perspectives concerning the role of adults in the lives of youth.

Jean E. Rhodes
Editor

Gil G. Noam
Editor-in-Chief

Enduring and supportive mentoring relationships can powerfully influence the course and quality of adolescent lives. As mentoring continues to expand, community agencies are implementing alternatives to the traditional one-on-one mentoring mode. Such efforts may help to reach youth who might otherwise fall through the cracks.

1

The rhetoric and reality of youth mentoring

Jean E. Rhodes, Jean B. Grossman, Jennifer Roffman

RELATIONSHIP-BASED INTERVENTIONS, such as mentoring, apprenticeship, and advising programs, are a central feature of youth development programs in this country. Such interventions are intuitively appealing, and politicians, educators, and practitioners alike widely endorse them. Moreover, a growing number of studies suggest that thoughtfully developed relationship-based programs can lead to improvements in youth's academic and vocational performance, social skills, behavior, and employment. This chapter provides an overview of youth mentoring programs, examining the factors that account for their dramatic expansion and outlining some promising trends in relationship-based interventions.

NEW DIRECTIONS FOR YOUTH DEVELOPMENT, NO. 93, SPRING 2002 © WILEY PERIODICALS, INC.

Why mentoring?

The dramatic expansion of relationship-based interventions has been fueled by several factors, not the least of which are the changes in families, work demands, and communities. More children are growing up in single- or low-income families, whose smaller household incomes and lack of flexibility in schedules have resulted in parents' having less time to spend with children. At the same time, parental concerns about declining neighborhood safety have led parents to restrict children's informal access to the remaining network of neighborhood adults. The additional supervisory burdens placed on school system and community centers to care for more children beyond the confines of the school day have stretched the available adult resources very thin.[1]

Concurrently, researchers and practitioners have increasingly shifted their attention from the prevention of specific problems to a more general focus on positive aspects of youth development. Discouraged by the limited long-term effectiveness of problem-focused programming,[2] those in the youth services field have moved increasingly toward creating a coordinated sequence of positive experiences and providing key developmental supports and opportunities. This has led to heightened policy interest in long-standing organizations such as the YMCA, Boys and Girls Clubs of America, and Big Brothers Big Sisters of America. Instead of focusing on problems, adherents to a youth development philosophy have attempted to identify *developmental assets*, competencies and resources (including adult support) that enhance children's and adolescents' chances of positive development. In their synthesis of more than eight hundred research studies, Scales and Leffert concluded that youth's connections with caring adults accounted for a range of developmental benefits, including higher self-esteem, greater engagement and performance in school, reduced delinquency and substance abuse, and better mental health.[3]

Also fueling the interest in mentoring is the spate of recent evaluations that have suggested that high quality mentoring programs can facilitate relationships and improve the lives of children.[4] Those in the field often credit a large evaluation of Big Brothers Big Sisters of America as the impetus for an expansion of mentoring throughout the 1990s.[5] The study included approximately one thousand ten- to sixteen-year-olds who applied to a geographically diverse set of Big Brothers Big Sisters programs. Researchers randomly selected a control group and put them on a waiting list for eighteen months; a group of youth in the experiment were matched with a mentor for an average of twelve months. Although all the youth showed gradual increases in problem behaviors over time (as is common in youth of this age), the behavior of the youth with mentors deteriorated at a slower rate than that of youth in the control group. At follow-up, youth who had been matched with mentors reported lower levels of substance use, less physical aggression, and more positive parent and peer relationships, as well as higher scholastic competence, attendance, and grades than control youth.[5] These and related findings drew attention to the potential for relationship-based interventions to redress the pressing need for additional adult supervision in the lives of youth and led to a concerted call for such programs nationally. Although this volume covers a range of relationship-based approaches, this chapter's major focus is on youth mentoring.

Variations in mentoring

In traditional one-on-one community-based matches, such as those that are characteristic of Big Brothers Big Sisters programs, an adult is matched with an unrelated younger protégé, and the pair typically meets weekly for one to four hours. During these meetings, the adult provides guidance, instruction, and encouragement aimed at developing the competence and character of the protégé. Although the pairs typically engage in a wide variety of leisure- and career-oriented discussions and activities, the two people involved have considerable flexibility as to where, how often, and when they meet. Despite the benefits of this approach and the many public service campaigns that have been launched to attract potential volunteers, a chronic shortage of volunteers significantly limits the growth of one-to-one mentoring. Moreover, the flexibility of this approach, although welcome to some, intimidates others. To overcome these barriers, many programs are trying new approaches in the hopes of attracting and expanding the influence of new volunteers.

Site-based mentoring programs, one of the fastest growing forms of mentoring, require a commitment to meet only one hour a week at school or work. This form of mentoring requires less time and forethought on the mentor's part. Group mentoring, another emerging strategy, is intended to increase the number of children who have access to a caring adult. This format tries to spread the wealth by assigning more than one youth to a mentor. Researchers at Philadelphia's Public/Private Ventures and elsewhere currently are conducting several preliminary studies on these newer forms of mentoring to understand both what they are and what they offer and, further, to determine their potential to make significant contributions to the field by recruiting new groups of mentors, serving new groups of youth, and most importantly, providing youth with real benefits.[6,7] In the following sections, we will describe some of these variations and discuss their potential contributions to developmental programming.

Site-based approaches

Increasingly, youth development programs are moving away from less structured community-based programming and focusing their efforts instead on site-based approaches to mentoring. Nearly half of the current crop of mentoring programs are site-based, with more than 70 percent located in schools and the remainder in workplace, agency, and religious settings. School-based, group, and work-based programs all tend to attract volunteers who are older, less educated, and more likely to be members of ethnic minorities than those found in traditional programs, thus expanding the pool of mentors. Many mentors in group programs mention that they were not comfortable with the intimacy and nonstructured nature of traditional matches, preferring to have some distance from the family and home lives of these youth.

A brief look at school-based mentoring reveals reasons for its particular appeal. School-based programs tend to be about half as costly per youth as traditional mentoring programs, even when we add the value of in-kind school contributions, such as staff, insurance, and space. And beyond the cost savings, school-based mentoring appears to have several benefits. For example, schools are better able to draw on the knowledge, referrals, supervision, and support of the many adults who are already in the setting. This simplifies the program staff's task of forming and monitoring relationships, and some preliminary evidence shows that the relationships can positively affect academic outcomes.[6] In addition, mentors in school-based programs have discussed the convenience and familiarity of the school and its structure.

But school-based programs have drawbacks as well. By their nature, they link their matches to the academic calendar, so many programs suspend or even terminate service during the summer months. This limits their effectiveness in part because program impacts tend to accrue with time and because behavioral problems and difficulties often arise during the summer months. Thus, it is not surprising that Aseltine and colleagues recently found that the benefits of a school-based mentoring program did not persist beyond the duration of the school year.[8] Even during the school year, Herrera and colleagues found that school-based mentors spent about half as much time with youth as did community-based mentors (six hours per month, compared with twelve hours) and that the relationships also tended to be less intensive than their community-based counterparts.[7] The school-based structure may constrain the intensity and scope of meetings in ways that community-based relationships do not. Moreover, school-based mentors' tendency to focus on academics may draw them away from the kinds of social activities that help to build close bonds.

Group mentoring

Beyond expanding the pool of mentors through site-based programs, another way of addressing the dearth of volunteers is to place multiple youth with one volunteer. Indeed, 20 percent of the more than seven hundred programs that Public/Private Ventures surveyed considered themselves to be group-mentoring programs. Yet group mentoring is a rather vaguely defined concept, showing considerable variation in group size, the number of adults associated with a group, the amount of time that the group spends together, the fluidity of the members, and the activities in which they engage.[10] It appears that during the school year the average group meets fourteen hours per month (typically at the school), though fluctuations in attendance make it difficult to determine how this fourteen hours of group time compares to the average of six or twelve hours of school- and community-based mentoring. On the other hand, although the relationships are likely to be less intense, mentors in group settings can provide children with guidance and advice on interacting with peers and dealing with social conflict. This real-time assistance is not typical in one-to-one interactions. Thus, group mentoring may have social impacts that one-to-one mentoring does not.

E-mentoring

A growing number of e-mail mentoring organizations have also emerged in recent years, some of which provide exclusively on-line relationships, connecting on-line pen pals. Although some youth may be able to form trusting emotional connections on-line, many researchers doubt whether such ties can consistently emerge in the absence of the adult's physical presence or whether the relationship will be significant enough to influence the life of the children. The jury is still out: no studies to date have examined whether e-mail mentoring can effectively substitute for face-to-face interactions. Still, despite these misgivings, we feel that the Internet may have a vital role in mentoring; e-mail exchanges can serve as a useful adjunct to ongoing relationships. E-mail's convenience may be particularly important to working professionals who can use it to sustain contact between meetings.

Mentoring in perspective

Can we assume that these newer forms of mentoring have the same effects as earlier forms? The answer to this question is likely to depend on the level of infrastructure and support that the program provides. As pointed out by much of the work by Public/Private Ventures and by DuBois and his colleagues in this volume, not all programs are equal. Programs without strong screening, training, and supervision tend to have relatively modest, if not neutral or negative, impacts. All programs try to provide adult support to youth, but issues of how often and for how long the mentor meets with the child, what they do, and where they meet differ greatly. Thus, we should use caution in generalizing the findings from Public/Private Ventures's landmark outcome study to other programs. Most Big Brothers Big Sisters affiliates require a year's commitment of their volunteers. Many other programs have shorter commitment periods. In a survey of more than seven hundred mentoring programs, Public/Private Ventures found that only 40 percent of other programs required a twelve-month commitment, and a third stated no understandings of minimum commitment.[9]

How effective are traditional mentoring programs?

Because mentoring programs vary so widely, definitive conclusions regarding mentoring's overall effectiveness are elusive. What does appear to be clear, however, is that the high level of enthusiasm among policymakers and practitioners for mentoring as a whole is not commensurate with evidence. For example, after reviewing the current literature, Freedman concluded that volunteer mentoring programs with disadvantaged youth are, for the most part, a "modest intervention."[10] Similarly, DuBois, Holloway, Cooper, and Valentine recently conducted a meta-analysis of fifty-five evaluations of mentoring programs and found the effects of the typical mentoring program to be relatively small, particularly when compared to other interpersonal interventions designed to improve youth outcomes.[11] They attributed the relatively small effect size (that is, the magnitude of program benefits) to wide variations in program quality. Expanding on earlier work by Public/Private Ventures,[6,7,12] the DuBois team has revealed a range of program practices that were associated with stronger effects, including training for mentors, structured activities for mentors and youth, more frequent contact, the support and involvement of parents, and the monitoring of overall program implementation in order to establish close relationships.

Two recent strands of research shed light onto the program practices that may be associated with successful mentoring and should be encouraged. One set of studies links the effectiveness of mentoring to the quality of the relationship between the pair and the duration of the bond.[13,14] The second links the quality and duration of relationships to screening, training, support for the pairing, and other best practices.[7,15] In other words, programs that are better run have in place the supports that enable mentors and youth to form relationships that are of higher quality and longer lasting, which in turn lead to youth deriving more positive benefits from the match. The research that has investigated the link between the quality of the relationship and its impacts has found that youth's perceptions of relationships are reliable predictors of outcome. Interestingly, youth tended to define close mentoring relationships less in terms of positive attributes than by the absence of negative interaction, such as being made to feel silly and ashamed.[14]

Going the distance

Given that a strong relationship seems to be the active ingredient of mentoring, it should come as no surprise that the effects of this intervention tend to emerge only over a relatively long period of time. Grossman and Rhodes explored the predictors and effects of relationship duration, testing the hypothesis that the effects of mentoring would grow stronger over time and that relatively short matches would lead to negative outcomes.[16] Youth who were in relationships that lasted a year or longer reported improvements in academic, psychosocial, and behavioral outcomes. Progressively fewer effects emerged among youth who were in relationships that terminated between six months and a year or between three and six months. Additionally, adolescents who were in relationships that terminated within a very short period of time reported decrements in several indicators of functioning. These observations underscore the need for careful screening and training of mentors and for the provision of ample resources to support the development and management of mentoring programs. Far more infrastructure to sustain mentoring programs exists now than in the past, but more is still needed.

Beyond mentoring programs

Of course, mentoring programs are not the only means by which relationships between caring nonparent adults and youth are forged. As Hamilton and Hamilton point out, apprenticeship programs enable employers to provide work-based learning opportunities for adolescents. Such programs have drawn considerable attention from policymakers and researchers and are considered a necessary response to the needs of youth who are both out of school and out of work. Youth with limited formal schooling, particularly those from low-income and minority communities, face substantial barriers to employment. They are often ill equipped to take on available jobs, which require increasingly high levels of education and skills, and spend the better part of their twenties somewhat adrift (see Hamilton and Hamilton, Chapter Three, this volume). When adolescents work with mature role models, they can acquire relevant workplace skills and learn both how to work and learn effectively in the nonschool world.

Beyond developing and strengthening relationship-based programs, however, additional strategies for encouraging relationships between adolescents and caring adults deserve consideration. As the articles in this volume make abundantly clear, meaningful relationships between adults and adolescents can occur in many contexts, ranging from highly structured arranged relationships to the more spontaneous yet influential ties that sometimes arise with teachers, advisers, and other adults. Such relationships have certain advantages over those arranged through programs. Adults from within youth's extended reach may be more familiar with the cultural norms, circumstances, and constraints of the setting and thus better positioned to offer credible advice. As such, mentoring and apprenticeship programs should be considered components of an

array of programs and activities that bring caring adults and adolescents together. Within this context, relationship-based interventions serve the broader goal of creating mentor-rich settings, in
which intergenerational relationships can thrive.

School systems

School systems are an obvious context for adolescents to develop
meaningful ties with adults. Relationships with certain teachers
sometimes can take on great importance during adolescence. Yet, as
Pianta, Stuhlman, and Hamre argue (Chapter Four, this volume),
schools could do much more to build into their operational blueprints strategies that foster close relationships. School- and
classroom-level practices that enrich student-teacher relationships
can enhance the well-being of middle school students. Even when
such practices are in place, however, many children fall through the
cracks. To address the needs of such youth, advising programs have
proliferated in many schools as an institutional antidote to the lack
of opportunities for students to form close relationships with teachers. As Rappaport points out in Chapter Five (this volume), however,
the quality of such programs is uneven as schools waver between, on
the one hand, embracing the challenges of forging close ties between
students and teachers, and on the other, treating the advising relationship as an extended homeroom period or study hall.

Conclusion

Like other relationships, those between individuals of two generations can vary along a continuum: some may be extraordinarily
helpful, whereas others can be marginally satisfying or even hurt-
ful. Obviously, we want to minimize harmful adult-youth relationships, but beyond that, we must recognize that different children
have different developmental needs. Certain youth might be
responsive only to highly structured, one-to-one relationships,
whereas others are perfectly adept at eliciting support from adults

in informal group contexts. Similarly, some need to work through difficulties of emotional adjustment, whereas other youth need help primarily in relating to peers or coping with schoolwork. A one-size-fits-all relationship intervention would be inappropriate for many children and adolescents, especially given that the supply of volunteers for the more intensive forms of mentoring is limited. Thus, it is promising that mentoring programs are in the process of diversifying.

Nonetheless, to assume that all of these newer types of relationships will offer the same benefits as the well-run, community-based, one-to-one mentoring programs that researchers have studied most intensively is shortsighted. As in traditional mentoring programs, the presence of a program infrastructure that promotes the development and maturation of strong positive relationships between youth and their mentors is likely to be critical to the effectiveness of the newer forms of mentoring. One fact, however, is certain. Today, many at-risk children and adolescents are falling through the cracks because not enough resources are available for them. A strong and pressing need exists for more research on the rapidly emerging forms of mentoring, many of which may hold the key to reaching more of these youth and making a difference in their lives.

Notes

1. Putnam, R. D. (2000). *Bowling alone: The collapse and revival of American community*. New York: Simon & Schuster.

2. Walker, G., & Vilella-Velez, F. (1992). *Anatomy of a demonstration: The Summer Training and Education Program (STEP) from pilot through replication and postprogram impacts*. Philadelphia: Public/Private Ventures.

3. Scales, P. C., & Leffert, N. (1999). *Developmental assets: A synthesis of the scientific research on adolescent development*. Minneapolis, MN: Search Institute.

4. Rhodes, J. E. (in press). *Stand by me: Risks and rewards in youth mentoring*. Cambridge, MA: Harvard University Press.

5. Grossman, J. B., & Tierney, J. P. (1998). Does mentoring work? An impact study of the Big Brothers/Big Sisters. *Evaluation Review, 22*, 403–426.

6. McClanahan, W. S. (1998). *Relationships in a career mentoring program: Lessons learned from the Hospital Youth Mentoring Program*. Philadelphia: Public/Private Ventures.

7. Herrera, C., Sipe, C. L., & McClanahan, W. S., with Arbreton, A. J., & Pepper, S. (2000). *Mentoring school-age children: Relationship development in*

community-based and school-based programs. Philadelphia: Public/Private Ventures.

8. Aseltine, R. H., Dupre, M., & Lamlein, P. (2000). Mentoring as a drug prevention strategy: An evaluation of Across Ages. *Adolescent and Family Health, 1*(1), 11–20.

9. Sipe, C. L., & Roder, A. E. (1999). *Mentoring school-age children: A classification of programs.* Philadelphia: Public/Private Ventures; Arlington, VA: National Mentoring Partnership.

10. Freedman, M. (1993). *The kindness of strangers: Adult mentors, urban youth, and the new volunteerism.* San Francisco: Jossey-Bass.

11. DuBois, D. L., Holloway, B. E., Cooper, H., & Valentine, J. C. (in press). Effectiveness of mentoring programs for youth: A meta-analytic review. *American Journal of Community Psychology.*

12. Sipe, C. L. (1996). *Mentoring: A synthesis of P/PV's research: 1988–1995.* Philadelphia: Public/Private Ventures.

13. Grossman, J. B., & Johnson, A. (1998). Assessing the effectiveness of mentoring programs. In J. B. Grossman (Ed.), *Contemporary issues in mentoring* (pp. 25–47). Philadelphia: Public/Private Ventures.

14. Reddy, R., Roffman, J. G., Grossman, J. B., & Rhodes, J. E. (2002). *Absence of malice: The development and validation of a youth mentoring relationship inventory.* Manuscript in preparation.

15. Stanwyck, D. A., & Anson, C. A. (1989). *The Adopt-a-Student evaluation project: Final report.* Atlanta: Georgia State University, Department of Educational Foundations.

16. Grossman, J. B., & Rhodes, J. E. (in press). The test of time: Predictors and effects of duration in youth mentoring programs. *American Journal of Community Psychology.*

JEAN E. RHODES *is associate professor in the Department of Psychology at the University of Massachusetts-Boston.*

JEAN B. GROSSMAN *is senior vice president for research at Public/Private Ventures and lecturer at Princeton University.*

JENNIFER ROFFMAN *is a postdoctoral research fellow in the Department of Psychology at the University of Massachusetts-Boston.*

Mentoring programs are effective only when mentors become significant adults in the lives of youth. Mentors who achieve this status provide support that helps youth develop important psychological and behavioral assets, such as self-esteem and the ability to cope, thus promoting healthy adjustment. These processes are evident in findings of an evaluation of outcomes in a Big Brothers Big Sisters of America program.

2

Testing a new model of mentoring

David L. DuBois, Helen A. Neville,
Gilbert R. Parra, Aalece O. Pugh-Lilly

RECENT ESTIMATES indicate that as many as one in five youth suffer from an emotional or behavioral disorder.[1] The costs for both youth and society of such difficulties are extensive, ranging from use of expensive services in childhood and adolescence (such as psychological testing and counseling) to continuation of problems at later stages of development.[2] Although prevailing approaches to prevention and treatment exhibit encouraging signs of effectiveness,[3] they fail to fully address the needs of youth. Many

Note: This research was supported by a grant to the first and second authors from the University of Missouri Research Board. The authors would like to thank volunteers, staff, and board members of Big Brothers Big Sisters of Boone County (Columbia, Mo.) for their support of this research; and Lisa Jones, Toby Lamb, Kris Mosakowski, Shivani Nanda, Shannon Prindiville, Elizabeth Sainz, Mary Starke, and Sharon Walker for their help collecting data.

NEW DIRECTIONS FOR YOUTH DEVELOPMENT, NO. 93, SPRING 2002 © WILEY PERIODICALS, INC.

prevention programs, for example, seek to increase levels of parental involvement and guidance, yet parents have a growing number of competing demands on their time. Likewise, professionals providing treatment are restricted in what they can offer to youth in need. Counselors or therapists can spend only a limited amount of time with any individual child, and they typically cannot interact with them outside of treatment.

Mentoring programs

Because of this need for greater availability of adult guidance and support, mentoring programs for youth have become increasingly popular. Currently, more than forty-five hundred organizations in the United States support mentoring activities.[4] Affiliates of Big Brothers Big Sisters alone now account for over five hundred mentoring programs nationwide. The National Mentoring Partnership and numerous other organizations also have contributed to significant growth in mentoring at local, state, and national levels.[5] The common denominator in these initiatives is the goal of fostering one-on-one relationships between youth and adult volunteers.

The effectiveness of mentoring programs

Despite burgeoning enthusiasm for mentoring programs, objective evaluations of their impact offer a more sobering perspective.[6] Findings of a recent meta-analysis of mentoring program evaluations are particularly noteworthy.[7] This synthesis of all available studies in the literature revealed that program participation typically does not result in substantial benefits for the emotional, behavioral, or academic adjustment of youth. Noteworthy benefits were apparent, however, when programs engaged in a majority of best practices (see Table 2.1).[8] Programs that specifically target disadvantaged youth also have yielded more favorable results. These types of program-level considerations are clearly very important. Yet even within any given well-designed program, some youth ben-

Table 2.1. Mentoring program best practices

Practice	Theory Based	Empirically Based
Monitoring of program implementation	X	X
Setting for mentoring activities[a]		X
Screening of prospective mentors	X	
Mentor background: helping role or profession		X
Mentor-youth matching	X	
Mentor prematch training	X	
Expectations: frequency of contact	X	X
Expectations: length of relationship	X	
Supervision	X	
Ongoing training	X	X
Mentor support group	X	
Structured activities for mentors and youth	X	X
Parent support or involvement	X	X

Note: Based on findings from a meta-analysis of the effectiveness of youth mentoring programs (DuBois et al., in press). Greater numbers of each type of practice predicted more positive outcomes for youth in mentoring programs. Theory-based practices are those that have been emphasized in the mentoring literature (for example, National Mentoring Working Group, 1991). Empirically based practices are those that predicted stronger outcomes in the meta-analysis.

[a]Programs in community and other settings outside of school (for example, in the workplace) yielded more favorable outcomes.

efit greatly from their involvement, whereas others experience little or no positive consequences.[4] For this reason, a simple input-output model in which participation in a mentoring program leads directly to improvements in adjustment for youth seems untenable (see Figure 2.1).

A new model of mentoring

The development of a significant bond between youth and mentor seems likely to be a necessary condition for positive outcomes to occur within mentoring programs, but a mentoring program's assignment of a volunteer does not necessarily ensure that the adult will be significant or influential in the youth's life. Strong mentor-youth relationships provide an opportunity for youth to receive social support from an extrafamilial adult role model. This support

Figure 2.1. Conceptual models of effects of youth mentoring programs on emotional and behavioral adjustment

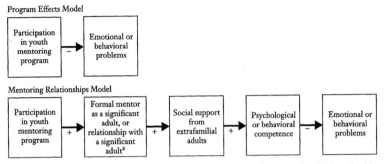

Program Effects Model

Mentoring Relationships Model

^a*Significant adult* refers to an individual (not a parent or other caregiver) identified by the youth in an open-ended nomination process.

may serve as a vehicle through which youth develop important psychological and behavioral assets, including self-esteem and abilities for coping. Such internalized resources seem to be the most noteworthy and enduring healthy outcomes for youth. The model of mentoring program effectiveness that we propose takes into account the intervening conditions and processes that are most likely to produce positive change (see Figure 2.1).

Mentors as significant adults in the lives of youth

Current empirical literature supports the view that characteristics of the relationship formed between youth and their mentors are an important source of variability in program outcomes.[4] In the meta-analysis we referred to previously,[7] a subset of nine studies compared outcomes for youth within programs according to the intensity and quality of their relationships with mentors. Youth identified as having enjoyed relatively strong relationships with their mentors were found to fare substantially better on a variety of outcome measures. Several methodological and conceptual issues, however, complicate interpretation of these findings. Some studies have used nominations from teachers or program staff to identify effective mentors.[9,10] Other researchers have reviewed mentor visit reports or logs to assess relationship quality.[11,12] But a significant concern with such approaches is that researchers' ratings of mentoring effectiveness may have been biased by their additional knowledge concerning the adjustment status of youth. That is, assessments of the quality of mentoring may have been influenced by the youth's outcomes.[7]

Further, only a few studies have taken into account the manner in which youth themselves experience their relationships with mentors. None of the outcome variables we noted previously, for example, provides for this type of assessment, nor do other investigations in which the focus has been on factors such as relationship longevity or frequency of mentor-youth contact.[13,14] Findings from related areas of research highlight the potential value of directly considering the experiences of youth with their mentors. In the psychotherapy and counseling literature, for example, the therapist-client relationship as perceived and reported on by clients is one of the strongest predictors of treatment outcomes.[15] The social support literature has similarly found it important to consider how individual children and adolescents perceive the quality of their ties with support providers.[16]

Promising results have also been reported in the limited research that has sought to link youth perspectives on mentoring relationships to program outcomes. Grossman and Rhodes found, for example, that youth perceptions of higher quality relationships with mentors in Big Brothers Big Sisters programs were related to greater duration of relationships, a factor that predicted more positive gains on several measures of adjustment.[17] Similarly, among students participating in the Adopt-A-Student Program,[18] those who reported high levels of support from their mentors were significantly more likely to be employed at follow-up than were those who reported low levels of support. Finally, students in the Sponsor-A-Scholar Program who viewed their mentoring relationships more positively were found to perform significantly better in terms of high school grades and first-year college attendance.[19] Interestingly, Johnson's study asked mentors a parallel set of questions to obtain their views of relationships, and overall, analyses using mentor-report data yielded results that were less consistent and informative than analyses using youth-report data. Findings thus provide support for the distinctive importance of youth perspectives on the quality of their mentoring relationships.

Several additional studies have examined youth perceptions of *natural mentors*, nonparent or nonpeer support figures. In these investigations, researchers have used open-ended procedures in which youth nominate natural mentors in their lives. Rhodes and colleagues found that adolescent mothers with mentors reported lower levels of depression and anxiety than those without mentors.[20,21] Adolescents with natural mentors also reported greater amounts of overall satisfaction with social support in each study. In a study of youth attending inner-city Boys and Girls Clubs of America, Hirsch and colleagues similarly found that perceptions of support from staff nominated as mentors predicted lower levels of psychological symptoms.[22] The use of an open-ended nomination technique in these studies is innovative and thus could offer certain advantages if incorporated into evaluations of youth mentoring programs. To date, studies have asked youth only whether they are willing to endorse mentors and their relationships with them as having various positive features. Similar impressions, if obtained through a less prompted or directed nomination process, could reflect the presence of more meaningful and valid ties. A nomination process is well suited to identifying ties with significant adults who may serve as natural mentors for youth in comparison or control groups. As we illustrate later in this chapter, such data provide a valuable opportunity to examine the presence of a significant adult or mentorlike figure as a general mechanism contributing to positive youth outcomes.

Contributions to psychological and behavioral competence

When mentors and youth develop significant bonds, the most direct benefit may be an increase in the overall social support available to youth from extrafamilial adults. Mentors and other adults may function as important sources of assistance to youth when they encounter stress or adversity. Yet such individuals will not always be present or easily accessible when help is needed, nor may relationships be sustained throughout all formative stages of a youth's development. This is especially true in the case of those relationships arranged through programs. Mentoring programs seldom ask for more than a one-year commitment from adult volunteers, for example, and in reality many relationships have even shorter durations.[4] A more substantial and enduring benefit of support from mentors may be its capacity to foster growth in the personal resources or skills of youth. Such resources have the potential to promote positive development even when significant adult figures are not accessible or no longer an active part of the youth's life.

Social support from mentors may help both to satisfy fundamental psychological needs of developing youth and to stimulate growth in age-appropriate behavioral competencies such as coping skills.[23] One of the most important psychological resources that mentoring promotes may be the youth's sense of self-worth. Supportive mentors may enhance the self-esteem of youth directly through unconditional positive regard as well as feedback that emphasizes the youth's strengths and positive abilities. They may also do so indirectly by serving as a reliable source of companionship, offering assistance with important practical concerns (such as schoolwork), and simply taking the time to listen to and validate the youth's feelings. Previous research has found that when youth receive social support from family, peers, and other natural support providers, one of the beneficial outcomes is an increase in their self-esteem.[24,25]

One important role of mentors may be to help youth acquire effective coping skills. In the process of helping youth negotiate differing types of stressors, mentors may model and instruct youth in skills and techniques that they can apply in similar situations. Available findings indicate that social support can indeed facilitate the use of active and problem-focused coping efforts among youth.[26] These coping tendencies are generally predictive of more positive mental health outcomes for youth.[27] The specific role of mentors in promoting adaptive coping behavior, however, has not been explored.

Taken together, these considerations guided development of the proposed model (see Figure 2.1). The model assumes that, as a basic condition for positive outcomes, the youth must perceive the program mentor as a significant adult in his or her life. One particularly important mechanism of effectiveness may be that programs increase the likelihood of youth having a relationship with at least one extrafamilial adult that they experience as significant and important.[4] Those relationships with mentors that youth identify spontaneously as having such status are presumed to offer the greatest benefits. Notably, this portion of the model also allows for the possibility that ties with naturally occurring mentors, when available, in the lives of youth may serve a similar function.

As the model indicates, we assume that a primary benefit of significant relationships with mentors is their capacity to enhance youth perceptions of the overall social support available to them from extrafamilial adults. This aspect of the model is consistent with findings from the social support literature referred to previously—that is, perceived quality of support, although tied to the presence of relevant persons in the youth's social network, is the more proximal source of influence on outcomes.[16] Such support is posited to promote youth's psychological and behavioral competence (such as self-esteem and coping skills). Increases in these resources then have a direct and positive influence on the susceptibility of youth to developing emotional and behavioral problems.[23] Overall, the model thus depicts a series of linkages through which participation in a mentoring program can have a favorable impact on the adjustment of any given youth.

Factors that promote the development of mentors as significant adults

As we have stressed, the most important link in the chain of influences is whether or not youth come to regard their mentors as significant adults in their lives. But what factors facilitate the development of this type of relationship? Demographic and background characteristics of mentors and youth such as gender, age, and ethnicity clearly merit consideration. These types of characteristics, however, have exhibited only limited patterns of association with process or outcome measures in evaluations of youth mentoring programs.[28] In the meta-analysis we referred to previously,[7] demographic characteristics of youth or mentors were found to be unrelated to the strength of program effects. This was true both when researchers considered such characteristics and when they examined their use as a basis for matching mentors and youth.

A more likely set of influential factors comes from the process-oriented aspects of mentoring relationships. Two dimensions of relationships highlighted as important in prior research are (1) the regularity and frequency of contact between mentors and youth[29,30,31] and (2) the longevity of the relationships.[17] Specific types of interactions and experiences seem also to contribute to the overall quality of relationships.[9,31,32] These include the types of activities that mentors and youth engage in together, the topics that they discuss, their mutual feelings of closeness, and any efforts they devote to addressing specific areas of concern such as the youth's self-esteem or schoolwork.

Establishing strong ties with youth often may be a demanding and time-consuming enterprise for mentors.[4] Use of appropriate screening procedures in programs, combined with adequate training and support mechanisms, can be keys to ensuring that mentors are equipped for this task.[4,7,33] Yet ultimately, individual mentors must assume responsibility for the development of their relationships with youth. Mentors with a strong sense of confidence and personal efficacy may have an easier time of this.[34] A greater sense of efficacy (and underlying skills and knowledge) with respect to issues involved in mentoring specifically could promote greater adaptive persistence when mentors encounter obstacles in developing relationships with youth. In this way, perceived self-efficacy has the potential to be instrumental in helping some mentors establish themselves as significant adults in the lives of youth.

Empirical study

We used data from an evaluation of a youth mentoring program to conduct an initial test of the proposed Mentoring Relationships

Model (see Figure 2.1). This model assumes the critical importance of taking into account the role of mentors as significant adults in the lives of youth when evaluating effects of programs. Compare the simpler Program Effects Model in which mentoring program participation leads directly to reductions in the emotional and behavioral problems of youth. A final set of analyses examines the extent to which youth and mentor demographic characteristics, relationship experiences reported by youth and mentors, and related factors are useful in helping to predict which program mentors youth will nominate as significant adults.

Methodology

The host agency for the research was an affiliate of Big Brothers Big Sisters, located in a midwestern city with a population of seventy thousand. The mission of the agency is to provide supportive one-on-one relationships in which adults serve as role models to youth and assist in their personal development (detailed descriptions of the agency are available[33]). Consistent with the agency's national guidelines, the unpaid volunteer mentors were expected to spend three to six hours per week with youth and maintain relationships for at least one year.

Sample and procedures

Participants included sixty-seven youth receiving mentors through the Big Brothers Big Sisters program (*program group*) and sixty-seven demographically matched youth who were not (*comparison group*). Youth in the program group included thirty boys and thirty-seven girls, ranging in age from seven to fifteen years ($M = 10.39$; $SD = 2.32$), and were either white ($n = 25$, 37.3 percent) or black ($n = 42$, 62.7 percent). Most of the youth lived in homes with a single adult caregiver ($n = 56$, 83.6 percent); a substantial majority also had low-income family backgrounds with annual reported income of $20,000 or less ($n = 48$, 71.6 percent). As a result of matching procedures, the comparison group was identical to the program group in terms of gender and racial or ethnic background and highly similar with respect to each of the following remaining matching variables: age (M = 10.72; SD = 2.41), single adult caregiver (n = 53, 79.1 percent), and low-income family background (n = 48, 68.7 percent).[1]

The Big Brothers Big Sisters mentors were the same gender as the youth whom they mentored, with the exception that in two instances a male-and-female couple jointly mentored a male youth. Mentors ranged in age from eighteen to fifty-six (M = 27.49; SD = 8.28),[2] and were either white (n = 54, 80.6 percent) or black (n = 13, 19.4 percent; all black mentors were matched with black youth). Eight mentors were married, although only one reported having a child who lived in the home; the overwhelming majority (approximately 90 percent) reported having obtained at least some postsecondary education.

We invited youth in the program group to participate in the study shortly before they were matched with mentors through Big Brothers Big Sisters. For seventy-two of ninety youth matched by the agency, parents gave consent for participation, and youth assented. The research did not include youth at the first-grade level or lower in school because of concerns regarding their ability to complete study measures appropriately. We collected data at six-month and one-year follow-up assessments from program group youth, regardless of whether the youth's relationships with his or her Big Brother or Big Sister remained active. Five youth are not included in the present analyses because their relationships with mentors ended prior to the conclusion of the research, and they or their parents or guardians elected to discontinue participation in the study at that time.

We recruited comparison group youth from the public school system in the community in which the Big Brothers Big Sisters agency was located. At the time each program group youth entered the study, we identified students in the school system who were of the same gender, age, grade in school, and racial or ethnic group, and who had comparable family composition (for example, single parent) and family income level. In instances in which we determined two or more youth to be a suitable match, we selected one randomly to participate in the research. The combined parent or guardian consent and youth assent rate for the comparison group was approximately 75 percent.

We collected data on three occasions or time points: time 1, at the time of matching with a mentor for program group and time of enrollment into the study for comparison group youth; time 2, six months after the match; and time 3, one year after the match. At each time point, youth completed questionnaires during interviews with trained research staff, who were not affiliated with the program agency. A parent or guardian and one of the youth's current teachers completed additional measures at each of the three time points. To provide for ongoing assessment of mentoring relationships and their development, we also conducted monthly telephone interviews. These were carried out separately with program group youth and their mentors throughout the one-year period.

Measures

Program outcomes. We assessed as program outcomes levels of emotional and behavioral problems that youth exhibited, measuring these using the subscales of the youth-, parent-, and teacher-report versions of the well-validated Achenbach checklist.[35] To reduce inaccuracies or bias associated with reports of any given informant, we standardized and averaged scale scores for all informants to form composite measures of emotional and behavioral problems, respectively, at each time point.[35]

Program mediating processes. We asked youth in both the program and comparison groups at each time of assessment whether they had any significant adults in their lives (other than parents or other primary caregivers), based on the following description:[21] "Significant adults are persons you count on and that are there for you, believe in and care deeply about you, inspire you to do your best, and influence what you do and the choices you make." Youth were to identify any such individuals according to the roles that they had in their lives (for example, Big Brother or Big Sister mentor, grandparent, and so on). To assess perceived social support available from these specific adults, youth completed ten items from a well-validated measure of perceived social support.[36] Examples include "The *significant adults* in my life notice and give me help when I need them to" and "I wish the *significant adults* in my life were nicer to me." Youth rated the items on a three-point response scale (not true, somewhat or sometimes true, very true or often true) and then scored from zero to three in the direction of greater perceived support and summed (coefficient alphas > .78 for both program and comparison groups at each time point). Consistently less than 15 percent of the overall sample of youth did not report any significant adults at any given time point. For these youth, we made a conceptually based decision to assign to them a score that corresponded to the lower end of the observed range of scores on the measure at the relevant time of assessment.

We assessed self-esteem and coping skills as indicators of psychological and behavioral competence, respectively. We assessed self-esteem using the Self-Esteem Questionnaire (SEQ), a well-validated measure for school-age children and adolescents.[37] Following prior research,[38] we used responses to this measure to construct a composite index of healthy and well-rounded self-esteem. This index corresponded to the average of three separate standardized indices derived from responses to the SEQ: overall feelings of self-worth (that is, Global Self-Esteem Scale); *profile level*, the average of scores on domain-specific scales of the measure, which target self-evaluations pertaining to peers, school, family, physical appearance, and sports or athletics; and *profile consistency*, as indexed by the inverse of the variance of scores across differing domains of self-evaluations. We assessed coping skills using the Self-Report Coping Scale (SRCS).[39] We averaged scores on the Problem-Solving and Seeking Social Support Scales of the SRCS to form a composite measure of approach-focused coping.[39]

Relationship experiences. We derived measures of relationship experiences separately from youth and mentor interview data (see Parra and colleagues for more detailed information on all measures[32]). Measures derived from monthly interviews assessed the frequency of youth-mentor contact during the month. They also assessed feelings of closeness, obstacles to relationship development (mentor report only), helpfulness of contacts with agency staff (mentor report only), types of activities engaged in and topics discussed, and perceived benefits for youth. The average of available monthly ratings served as a measure of the overall level of each type of relationship experience as reported by the youth or the mentor. In addition, we computed trends over time (or individual growth curves) on relationship measures for particular youth and mentors. For each measure, these were derived using a series of ordinary least-squares regression analyses in which time served as a linear predictor of the scores of differing youth and mentors on the relevant measure over the twelve monthly interviews.[40] Prior to using them as predictors in study analyses, we residualized the resulting slope estimates on the initial (month one) status of each youth and mentor on the corresponding measure. We did this to remove variance reflective of "regression to the mean" effects stemming from a relatively low or high starting point on any given measure.

Additional measures. We obtained several additional measures. At the time each youth and mentor were matched, we asked mentors to respond to a set of questions about the amount and quality of training they received from the agency. In addition, we asked them a series of questions about their sense of personal efficacy with regard to being able to function effectively as mentors. At the one-year assessment, both youth and mentors completed a fifteen-item measure assessing perceived benefits for the youth in specific areas (such as self-esteem, relationships with family members, and schoolwork). Finally, data on the longevity of all relationships during the one-year period (in months) were available. Forty-eight relationships lasted the entire twelve months. The others ended prior to this date and had an average length of approximately seven months ($M = 7.1$; $SD = 2.6$).

Involvement in other supportive services

To take into account the influence of supportive services other than the Big Brothers Big Sisters program (for example, counseling or therapy, special education), we asked parents of all participants at the initial assessment to report on their child's current involvement in these types of activities. We standardized the number of services reported and the average reported frequency of involvement in such activities on a seven-point scale and combined them to form a composite measure for use in study analyses.

Results

We conducted path modeling analyses using version 5.1 of the EQS computer program.[41] Separate path models were fit for both the Program Effects and Mentoring Relationships Models (see Figure 2.1). In each instance, an initial model was fit that included estimation of paths judged to be most theoretically relevant to the model involved. Using a model generation strategy,[42] we then examined Lagrange Multiplier modification indices to identify other paths that, if added to the model, would contribute significantly to overall fit (a test that is equivalent to evaluating the significance of the relevant path once included in the model); to avoid capitalization on chance (that is, Type I error), we used a conservative criterion of $p < .001$. We added these types of paths, furthermore, only when they were theoretically interpretable within the overall context of the model.[42] We then determined the final model by deleting any hypothesized paths that failed to reach or approach significance ($p < .10$).

The initial path models that we evaluated for each theoretical model included four exogenous variables:

- Group status (program = 1 versus comparison = 0)
- A dichotomous variable indicating whether a significant adult was nominated by the youth at time 1 (1 = yes; 0 = no; nominations of recently matched Big Brothers or Big Sisters mentors were excluded for youth in program group)
- Time 1 measures of perceived support from significant adults and involvement in other supportive services
- Time 1 composite measures of emotional and behavioral problems

Preliminary analyses (that is, independent groups' t tests) did not reveal any significant associations between program versus comparison group status and the other five exogenous measures.

Each initial path model also shared several other features: (1) estimation of covariances among all exogenous measures (that is, involvement in the Big Brothers Big Sisters program and the five control measures), (2) estimation of covariances between error terms for measures of emotional and behavioral problems at time 2 and 3, respectively, and (3) paths representing stability effects for emotional and behavioral problems from time 1 to time 2 and from time 2 to time 3, respectively.

Program Effects Model. To evaluate the Program Effects Model, a model was fit that included additional paths representing effects of both involvement in the Big Brothers Big Sisters program and relevant exogenous control measures (such as involvement in other supportive services) on levels of emotional and behavioral problems at times 2 and 3. The final model, obtained after considering possible additional paths and omitting those hypothesized that did not approach significance, is shown in Figure 2.2. Note that a path indicating an effect of involvement in the Big Brothers Big Sisters program on reduced behavioral problems at time 2 approached significance in this model. No other effects of program participation on outcomes were evident.[3]

Figure 2.2. Final path model for Program Effects Model

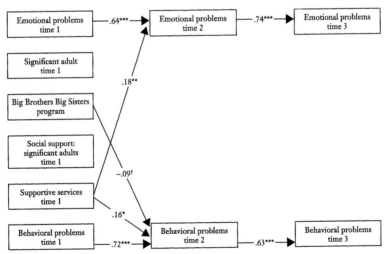

Note: Path coefficients are standardized, and significance levels were determined by critical ratios on unstandardized coefficients ($\dagger p < .10$; $^*p < .05$; $^{**}p < .01$; $^{***}p < .001$). Not depicted are correlations among exogenous measures, such as Big Brothers Big Sisters program involvement and all time 1 measures, as well as those between error (residual) terms for selected other measures. Overall model fit indices: $\chi^2(21) = 24.80$, $p = .26$; comparative fit index = .99; normed fit index = .97; nonnormed fit index = 99.

Mentoring Relationships Model. To evaluate the Mentoring Relationships Model, a model was fit in which involvement in the agency program had a direct influence on whether or not youth nominated a formal mentor (such as the Big Brother) as a significant adult at time 2 (1 = yes; 0 = no), controlling for similar possible influences of each of the other exogenous measures we noted previously. We then modeled nomination of a formal mentor as significant adult as influencing the overall level of perceived support from significant adults at time 2, which, in turn, had effects on time 2 indices of self-esteem and approach-focused coping. We then estimated the effects of the latter two measures on time 2 levels of emotional and behavioral problems. We modeled the same relations for measures at time 3. Further paths allowed for influences of each time 2 significant adult measure (nomination of a formal mentor and level of perceived support) on the corresponding measure at time 3 as well as an effect of time 2 perceived support from significant adults on whether a formal mentor was nominated as a significant adult at time 3 (mediating the direct effect of such a nomination at time 2). At both time points, we modeled effects of perceived support from significant adults on emotional and behavioral problems as being mediated entirely by their intermediary linkages with self-esteem and coping (that is, no direct effects of perceived support on these outcome measures).

Finally, to allow for shared variance in unexplained portions of measures of self-esteem and coping at each time point, we estimated the covariance between residual terms for these measures.

As shown in Figure 2.3, the final Mentoring Relationships Model provided a good overall fit to the data. Of particular note are the paths, shown in bold, that indirectly linked involvement in the agency program to reduced levels of both emotional and behavioral problems at times 2 and 3 (see Figure 2.2). These pathways begin with a substantial linkage between participation in the program and nomination of a formal mentor as a significant adult at time 2, with twenty-seven youth (40.3 percent) in the program group making this type of nomination, as opposed to only one youth in the control group (1.5 percent).[4] Similar numbers of youth made this type of nomination at time 3 (n = 25, 37.3 percent of the

Figure 2.3. Final path model for Mentoring Relationships Model based on nominations of significant adults

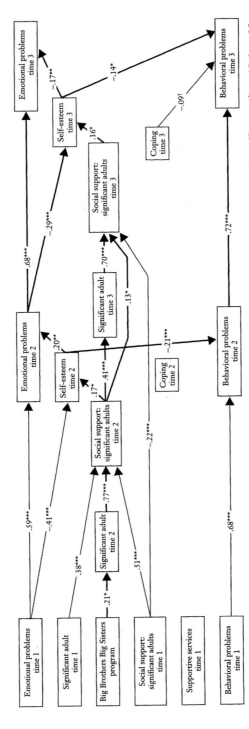

Note: Path coefficients are standardized, and significance levels were determined by critical ratios on unstandardized coefficients (†p < .10; *p < .05; **p < .01; ***p < .001). Paths accounting for indirect effects of Big Brothers Big Sisters program involvement on emotional and behavioral problems appear in bold. Not depicted in each model are correlations among exogenous measures, such as program involvement and all time 1 measures, as well as those between error (residual) terms for selected other measures. Overall model fit indices: $\chi^2(113) = 172.82$, $p < .001$; comparative fit index = .94; normed fit index = .86; nonnormed fit index = 92.

program group; $n = 2$, 3 percent of the comparison group). Among the program group, time 3 nominations were most likely for those youth who also had nominated their mentor as a significant adult at time 2 ($n = 15$, 55.5 percent, of these twenty-seven youth compared to $n = 10$, 25 percent, of the remaining forty youth). This pattern accounted for the significant path linking time 2 and time 3 nominations in the path model. At both times 2 and 3, nomination of a formal mentor was subsequently related to greater perceived social support from significant adults. Perceived support from significant adults then had positive effects on self-esteem at each time point. Self-esteem, in turn, was linked to lower levels of emotional and behavioral problems (see Figure 2.3).

Overall, we thus linked participation in the agency program through the expected series of intermediary effects to reductions in youth's levels of both emotional and behavioral problems. When testing these overall indirect effects within the model, we found involvement in the program to be linked significantly to fewer behavioral problems at time 2 ($p < .01$) and to fewer emotional and <.001, for each effect).[5]

An additional path analysis further investigated the Mentoring Relationships Model. In this model, nomination of a formal mentor at times 2 and 3 was replaced by variables that indicated whether each youth nominated any significant adult. The model thus evaluated whether involvement in the program increased the likelihood that youth would report having any type of extrafamilial significant adult in their lives. As can be seen in Figure 2.4, we obtained similar results as in the model that limited nominations to formal mentors. In particular, the paths shown in bold again linked program involvement to reductions in emotional and behavioral problems at times 2 and 3. Notably, these included a significant path indicating an effect of program involvement on greater likelihood of nomination of a significant adult at time 2. This path is accounted for by a higher proportion of youth in the program group nominating at least one significant adult (91.0 percent, $n = 61$) than those in the comparison group (80.6 percent, $n = 54$); the former group included nine youth who nominated only their Big Brother or Big

Figure 2.4. Final path model for Mentoring Relationships Model based on nominations of any significant adults

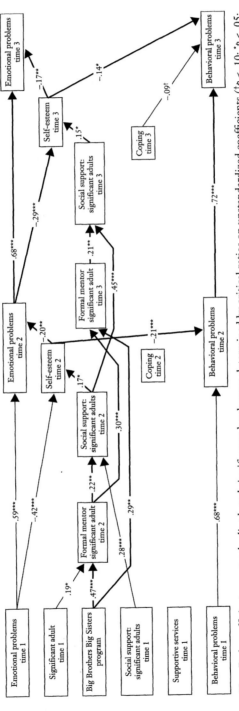

Note: Path coefficients are standardized, and significance levels were determined by critical ratios on unstandardized coefficients ($\dagger p < .10$; $^*p < .05$; $^{**}p < .01$; $^{***}p < .001$). Paths accounting for indirect effects of Big Brothers Big Sisters program involvement on emotional and behavioral problems appear in bold. Not depicted in each model are correlations among exogenous measures, such as program involvement and all time 1 measures, as well as those between error (residual) terms for selected other measures. Overall model fit indices: $\chi^2(113) = 205.38$, $p < .001$; comparative fit index = .93; normed fit index = .86; nonnormed fit index = 90.

Sister and an additional ten youth who identified this individual first in the process of nominating more than one significant adult. In this model, the linkage between nominations of a significant adult at times 2 and 3 was mediated by an effect of nomination at time 2 on level of perceived support from significant adults at the same time of assessment. All linkages of program involvement to reduced levels of emotional and behavioral problems, however, again involved effects of social support on self-esteem rather than coping. When evaluating overall indirect effects for this model, we found program involvement to be linked significantly to fewer behavioral problems at time 2 and to fewer emotional and behavioral problems at time 3 (p's < .05); in addition, the remaining indirect effect of program involvement on emotional problems at time 2 approached significance ($p < .09$) in this analysis.

Predicting nomination of Big Brothers Big Sisters program mentors as significant adults

The preceding analyses indicate that nomination of agency mentors as significant adults had a role in mediating program effects on outcomes. We were interested in examining whether such nominations varied in frequency according to demographic characteristics of mentors or youth and whether they could be predicted on the basis of measures of relationship experiences and related factors (such as mentor efficacy) described previously. We identified three groups of youth within the program group for this purpose: (1) *No Nomination*, youths who did not nominate a mentor at time 2 or time 3 (n = 30, 44.8 percent); (2) *Partial Nomination*, youths who nominated a mentor at one of the two time points but not both (n = 22, 32.8 percent); and (3) *Consistent Nomination*, youths who nominated a mentor at both time points (n = 15, 22.4 percent).

We conducted analyses first on a univariate basis. These investigated the extent to which group membership exhibited associations with individual mentor and youth demographic characteristics and with specific relationship measures. We conducted chi-square tests of associations for categorical demographic variables; we examined continuous measures using one-way analyses of variance with Student Newman-Keuls tests for pairwise group differences. Among demographic variables, gender of the youth was associated significantly with group membership ($2(2) = 7.14, p < .05$). Boys accounted for a substantially greater proportion of the Consistent Nomination group ($n = 11$, 73.3 percent) than did girls ($n = 4$, 26.7 percent); in a corresponding manner, girls made up a larger proportion of the No Nomination group (girls: $n = 20$, 66.7 percent; boys: $n = 10$, 33.3 percent).[6]

Numerous relationship measures derived from both youth-report and mentor-report data also varied significantly by group membership (see Table 2.2). These measures assessed frequency of contact, relationship closeness, involvement in differing types of activities and discussions, and perceived benefits for youth. Newman-Keuls follow-up tests revealed significant differences in the direction of higher or increasing (in the case of slope estimates) scores on these measures for youth in the Consistent Nomination group relative to those in the No Nomination group. In several instances, scores also were significantly higher or showed greater

Table 2.2. Differences on relationship measures in relation to nomination of Big Brother or Big Sister as a significant adult

	Group				
Measure	*No Nomination (NN)*	*Partial Nomination (PN)*	*Consistent Nomination (CN)*	*F*	*Newman-Keuls*[a]
	Youth Report				
Frequency of contact				6.07**	CN>NN
M	−0.27	0.06	0.37		
SD	0.57	0.53	0.68		
Relationship closeness				4.20*	CN>NN
M	5.65	6.00	6.54		
SD	1.23	0.79	0.46		
Relationship closeness (slope)				4.42*	CN,PN>NN
M	−0.13	0.08	0.11		
SD	0.42	0.14	0.07		
Activities: sports or athletic (slope)				5.21**	CN,PN>NN
M	−0.01	0.00	0.01		
SD	0.02	0.02	0.02		
Activities: recreational or nonathletic (slope)				6.29**	CN>PN,NN
M	−0.01	0.00	0.03		
SD	0.05	0.02	0.02		

Table 2.2. *continued*

Measure	No Nomination (NN)	Partial Nomination (PN)	Consistent Nomination (CN)	F	Newman-Keuls[a]
		Group			
Discussion: youth's behavior (slope)					
M	−0.03	0.02	0.04	3.86*	CN>NN
SD	0.12	0.05	0.05		
Discussion: youth's relationships (slope)					
M	−0.05	0.02	0.06	7.05**	CN,PN>NN
SD	0.14	0.06	0.05		
Discussion: casual conversation					
M	0.52	0.58	0.83	3.87*	CN>PN,NN
SD	0.35	0.34	0.36		
Discussion: casual conversation (slope)					
M	−0.04	0.02	0.05	5.88**	CN,PN>NN
SD	0.12	0.06	0.04		
Discussion: social issues					
M	0.15	0.11	0.31	4.10*	CN>PN,NN
SD	0.21	0.12	0.30		
Discussion: social issues (slope)					
M	−0.01	−0.01	0.03	8.27***	CN>PN,NN
SD	0.04	0.02	0.01		
Benefits for youth[b]					
M	5.30	5.98	6.48	7.62**	CN,PN>NN
SD	1.20	0.86	0.56		
Benefits for youth[c]					
M	3.32	3.82	3.96	3.21*	None
SD	1.03	0.72	0.81		
		Mentor Report			
Frequency of contact					
M	−0.23	0.00	0.55	5.35**	CN>PN,NN
SD	0.67	0.49	0.76		
Relationship closeness					
M	4.03	4.83	5.27	5.37**	CN,PN>NN
SD	1.38	0.76	0.87		
Activities: sports or athletic					
M	0.18	0.20	0.34	3.20*	CN>PN,NN
SD	0.15	0.17	0.21		
Activities: recreational or nonathletic					
M	0.48	0.60	0.75	4.56*	CN>NN
SD	0.26	0.20	0.23		
Benefits for youth[b]					
M	4.18	4.79	5.18	4.50**	CN,PN>NN
SD	1.18	0.75	0.60		

Note: $n = 65$ for youth-report measures; $n = 53$ for mentor-report measures.

[a]$p < .05$.

[b]Monthly benefits ratings.

[c]Year-end benefits ratings.

*$p < .05$. **$p < .01$. ***$p < .001$.

increases for the Consistent Nomination group relative to the Partial Nomination group or for the Partial Nomination group in comparison with the No Nomination group.

Next, we used discriminant function analysis to identify the variables that could most parsimoniously distinguish between youth in the three groups. We conducted separate analyses for youth-report and mentor-report measures, considering demographic variables in each analysis as well. We used a stepwise hierarchical method of variable selection. In particular, we considered five sets of variables sequentially for entry into the discriminant function: (1) demographic characteristics of youth or mentors, depending on whether we were considering youth- or mentor-report relationship measures; (2) mentor ratings of the quality of training, their perceived efficacy as mentors, and helpfulness of contacts with program staff (mentor-report analysis only); (3) frequency of mentor-youth contact and relationship longevity; (4) relationship experiences (mentor-report only); and (5) perceived benefits for youth. This ordering was intended to represent a progression from relatively distal to relatively more proximal influences on the quality and effectiveness of mentoring relationships.[32] As noted, we used a stepwise approach to variable selection and entry within each block of predictors. Specifically, for a variable to be entered, it needed to produce an increment in the amount of centroid separation that at least approached significant at a liberal threshold ($p < .15$).

In the analysis using youth-report relationship measures, we obtained one significant function (see Table 2.3). This function indicated that the most powerful multivariate discriminator was a profile that reflected the weighted addition of gender (with a positive weight for males); greater average levels of mentor-youth contact, relationship closeness, and discussion of social issues; and positive change over time in levels of engagement in sports or athletic activities as well as in discussions about the youth's relationships and social issues. This function discriminated significantly among all three possible pairings of the nomination groups (p's < .05), with those in the Consistent Nomination group scoring highest, followed by those in the Partial Nomination group. Overall,

Table 2.3. Discriminant analyses for groups differing in nomination of Big Brother or Big Sister as a significant adult

Variable	Analysis Using Youth-Report Measures	Analysis Using Mentor-Report Measures
	Standardized Coefficients	
Gender	.47	.53
Mentor efficacy	—	.86
Frequency of contact	.11	—
Frequency of contact (slope)	—	1.84
Relationship closeness	.51	—
Activities: sports or athletic (slope)	.46	—
Discussion: youth's relationships (slope)	.25	—
Discussion: social issues	.29	—
Discussion: social issues (slope)	.29	−1.17
Group	Centroids	
No Nomination	−0.82	−0.67
Partial Nomination	0.04	0.41
Consistent Nomination	1.48	0.94
Canonical R	.68**	.56*

Note: $n = 65$ for analysis using youth-report measures; $n = 53$ for analysis using mentor-report measures.

*$p < .01$. **$p < .001$.

the function correctly classified 64.1 percent of youth; it was particularly effective for distinguishing youth in the Consistent Nomination and Partial Nomination groups, considered together, from those in the No Nomination group (that is, 73.4 percent overall correct classification).

We also obtained one significant function in the analysis using mentor-report measures. This function represented the weighted addition of gender (again with a positive weight for males), greater ratings of mentor efficacy, positive change over time in frequency of mentor-youth contact, and negative change over time in reported frequency of discussion of social issues. This function discriminated the No Nomination group significantly from the Partial Nomination and Consistent Nomination groups (p's < .05) but did not differentiate significantly between the latter two groups ($p > .20$). Those in the Consistent Nomination group again scored highest on the function, followed by those in the Partial Nomination group. Overall, this function correctly classified 47.2 percent of youth, a relatively low figure; it was, however, notably more effective when used as a basis for distinguishing youth in the Consistent Nomination and Partial Nomination groups, considered together, from those in the No Nomination group (71.7 percent).

Discussion

In the present research, we found no significant direct effects of participation in a Big Brothers Big Sisters mentoring program on the emotional or behavioral adjustment of youth over a one-year period. Consistent with a recent meta-analysis of youth outcomes in mentoring programs,[7] findings thus fail to support a simple, input-output model (or Program Effects Model, see Figure 2.1). The host agency incorporated numerous empirically supported best practices into its programming efforts (see Table 2.1), including careful screening of prospective mentors, matching of mentors and youth on multiple criteria, clear guidelines or expectations for both frequency of contact and minimum duration of relationships, and initial training followed by supervision from agency staff to monitor relationship development. A majority of youth served by the agency were also from low-income family backgrounds, a factor associated with increased positive effects of mentoring.[7] These considerations underscore the reality that even well-designed mentoring programs delivered to appropriate populations offer no assurance of benefits for participating youth.[4]

Available research indicates a need to take into account the differing experiences that youth have in the quality and intensity of their relationships with mentors. For example, only approximately 40 percent of youth in the intervention group for the present sample spontaneously nominated their Big Brother or Big Sister as a significant adult in their lives either six months or one year after having been matched. Notably, we found these nominations to be the first link in a chain of associations that revealed indirect positive effects of program participation on levels of emotional and behavioral problems at both assessments. Nominations were linked to outcomes by way of intermediary effects on the level of perceived social support from significant adults, regardless of mentor source (that is, formal or informal).

In general, it appears that programs such as Big Brothers Big Sisters can be effective in enhancing the presence of adult support figures in youths' lives, even in periods as short as six months. Youth's perceptions of these adults' significance tend to be sustained over time, at least as far as we can discern within the one-year time frame of the current research.

In the model restricted to nominations of formal mentors as significant adults, the linkage between this type of nomination at the six-month and one-year assessments was direct and thus not mediated by intervening perceptions of increased social support. A direct path also linked participation in the agency program to nomination of a formal mentor as a significant adult at the one-year assessment. These findings indicate that support received from mentors in the relatively early stages of relationships is not the only or necessarily even primary mechanism accounting for the strong ties that youth report later. Rather, for some youth, what may be most important is simply the opportunity for the relationship to progress and grow. For that to happen, however, relationships must be sustained, which was not the case for over 25 percent of mentoring relationships in the program group. The direct link between youth's nominating formal mentors as significant adults across the early and later time points suggests that youth who feel that mentors are important persons in their lives will help maintain the relationships. This type of positive regard is likely to increase the receptiveness of youth to guidance and advice that the mentors offer, thus making it easier to cultivate strong bonds. Yet in some cases, youth can eventually see mentors as significant adults (for example, at one year in the present study) even when this appreciation is not apparent in the first stages of the relationship. This suggests that it may also be important for mentors to be able to persevere when initial signs of progress or rewards are limited. In previous research, stronger efficacy beliefs on the part of mentors predicted increased longevity of relationships.[32] Ratings of perceived efficacy were similarly higher in the present study for those mentors whom youth ultimately perceived to be significant support figures in their lives. Mentors' feelings of confidence and tendencies toward adaptive persistence thus seem valuable in helping them to establish strong connections with youth, perhaps especially when relationships need time to develop.

Findings differed somewhat when focusing on the presence of a significant adult more generally. Pathways linking program participation to greater likelihood of nomination as significant adult at the end of the one-year period were mediated entirely by relationship measures from the six-month assessment. Furthermore, rather than being direct, the linkage between nominations at the two time points occurred by way of an intermediary association involving the level of perceived support from significant adults. These findings indicate that mentoring programs can also be effective by initiating relatively immediate changes in the social support networks of youth, with such changes then being instrumental in helping to maintain relationships over time. The processes involved may closely resemble those accounting for favorable effects of natural mentoring relationships in the lives of youth.[20,21] Recall that most youth in the comparison group still nonetheless reported the presence of a significant nonparental adult in their lives; so too did a substantial number of those who were in the program but who failed to nominate the Big Sister or Big Brother. Thus, even though program involvement was associated with an increased likelihood of youth reporting the presence of a significant adult, it clearly was only one of many sources for such ties.

The preceding considerations suggest several implications for theory development as well as program design and evaluation. For theory, processes that are salient in natural mentoring relationships may also be important in the context of the ties that youth have with formal mentors assigned by programs.[6] Youth who develop significant ties with formal mentors, for example, may benefit from feeling attached to them and receiving guidance or advice in a manner similar to other supportive relationships with outside adults.[6] It also is relatively commonplace for natural mentors to be helped in their efforts by close ties with youths' parents, in part because they are often themselves members of an extended kin network.[43] These types of connections are less apt to exist within the context of formal mentoring. Yet recall that efforts to increase parental involvement in programs are associated with stronger outcomes for youth.[7]

Greater attention to facilitation of key components of natural mentoring would seem a promising avenue for the design of more widely effective programs. We might argue as well that programs are likely to be directed most profitably to those youth who currently lack any significant nonparental adults in their lives. Given lengthy waiting lists for youth seeking mentors in many programs, an agency might reasonably prioritize need by taking into account the availability of similar supports for a youth. For evaluation activities, this implies the need to do a better job of assessing the presence of natural mentors both among youth receiving program mentors and those in control or comparison groups.[7] It may be difficult otherwise, if not impossible, to be confident that observed effects on youth outcomes are attributable to programmatic efforts as opposed to mentoring taking place in other parts of youths' lives. In addition, as these findings illustrate, the potential exists for program effects to go undetected if information pertinent to a mediational role for both natural and formal mentors as significant adults is not available to be incorporated into analyses.

The present results also highlight a mediational role for psychological resources in reducing levels of emotional and behavioral problems in adjustment. This is consistent with the view that the effectiveness of community-based interventions for children and adolescents is derived in significant part from their ability to promote satisfaction of basic psychological needs.[23] This study focused on feelings of self-worth. Results indicate that social support provided by mentors and other significant adults tends to increase positive feelings of self-regard among youth, which can be an important mechanism leading to beneficial outcomes.[24] Bearing out earlier research,[25] this implies that effective mentoring is able to facilitate gains in self-esteem that enhance academic, emotional, and behavioral adjustment. The present research indicates that mentoring can enhance both the level and consistency of self-evaluations across multiple domains, including family, school, peers, and so on. Support from mentors and other significant adults may contribute to a healthy, well-rounded foundation for overall feelings of self-worth and thus strengthen esteem-mediated pathways to positive outcomes.[44] Supportive mentoring relationships are also likely to address other important psychological needs of youth, such as the desire for a sense of control and relatedness to others.[23] Consequently, psychologically mediated linkages with outcomes may be stronger than those for the current context, which measured only one type of need. Furthermore, despite a lack of evidence of mediating effects on use of active coping strategies, mentoring relationships theoretically can promote behavioral competence in a wide range of areas,[4] including social skills with peers and the capacity to adapt at home and school. Overall, psychological and behavioral mechanisms of influence represent one of the most promising avenues for advancing a process-oriented understanding of the effects of mentoring programs on youth.

A process-oriented view of mentoring relationships and their effectiveness also must be informed by consideration of specific patterns of activity and experiences that occur between mentors and youth. In the present research, a wide range of relationship measures helped distinguish between youth in the agency program who did and did not nominate their mentors as significant adults. As we expected, demographic characteristics of mentors and youth generally did not prove helpful for predicting outcomes. A notable exception, however, is that boys were approximately twice as likely as girls to nominate the mentor as a significant adult at some point in the study. A large majority of youth lived in female-headed, single-parent homes. Boys thus often did not have a same-sex adult role model available in their home environments, a factor that may have heightened their receptivity to forming close ties with male program mentors. Interestingly, a larger-scale evaluation of Big Brothers Big Sisters programs similarly reported that matches involving males were less likely to terminate than those involving females.[17] We previously emphasized the need, when investigating mentoring program effectiveness, to take into account youths' naturally occurring ties with extrafamilial adults. The present discussion illustrates the need for paying similar attention to ties with parental and other primary caregiving figures. Without such consideration, it may not be possible to arrive at an adequate understanding of the role and significance of a formal mentor in the life of any youth.

With regard to relationship measures, several aspects of the findings are noteworthy. First, taken together with previous research,[30,31,32] they underscore that not only the frequency of mentor-youth contact but also the nature of the interactions that characterize the relationship are important. Thus, even after accounting for a positive contribution of rate of contact in the present research, measures tapping feelings of closeness as well as levels of engagement in specific types of activities and discussions were found to further discriminate between youth who did and did not nominate mentors as significant adults. Second, prior studies have been limited primarily to static or onetime assessments of mentoring relationships. The current investigation demonstrates the usefulness of also considering indices of mentoring relationships' development and change over time. In general, youth may be most likely to come to regard mentors as significant adults in their lives when relationships show increasing levels of involvement and emotional intensity over time. One interesting implication is that it may be relatively ineffective or even counterproductive to place too much emphasis on certain features of relationships in their earliest stages.

A further aspect of results is that relationship measures from youth reports were more consistent and powerful predictors of nominations of mentors as significant adults than were corresponding indices based on mentor reports.[18] A youth perspective affords the opportunity to be sensitive to the manner in which children and adolescents may interpret or respond to interactions in ways that differ from their mentors. In the current research, for example, we found that youth who nominated their mentors as significant adults tended to report discussing social issues with them often and more frequently as their relationships developed; by contrast, mentor-report data showed a declining pattern of emphasis on discussion of social issues that was associated with greater likelihood of positive nominations from youth. The same examples of this type of conversation topic (for example, current events) were provided to both types of informants. Yet it is possible that youth viewed the term *social issues* somewhat more flexibly or broadly. Their focus, for example, might have been on conversations they had with mentors about social issues more directly in their sphere of personal interest, such as situations at school, and thus of greater concern to them. Developmental considerations as well as differences in the backgrounds of mentors and youth (for example, social class) could be responsible for such areas of divergence. Future work should investigate these. More generally, the mentoring literature could benefit from increased attention to a youth perspective on relationships for both theoretical and applied progress.

The process-oriented measures of relationships included in this research were least successful in being able to distinguish between youth who consistently nominated their mentors as significant adults and those who did so at just one of the two possible time points. Researchers may need to consider more in-depth or subtle qualities of relationships to optimally differentiate among ties between mentors and youth at the positive end of the continuum. Issues that we discussed in this chapter suggest, for example, that considering more carefully the role and significance of the mentoring relationship within the context of the youth's overall social network might be useful. This might entail examining such concerns as the availability of alternative sources of mentoring and whether beneficial ties exist between the mentor and other key persons in the youth's network. It is also important to consider the significance or appropriateness of differing mentor strategies in relation to the youth's age or developmental level. Some research indicates that giving youth choice over activities, for example, can be desirable in mentoring relationships.[31] Yet this strategy may well prove especially important when mentoring adolescents. Such possibilities underscore the broad range of factors that is likely to be involved in shaping ties between mentors and youth at differing points along a continuum of importance or effectiveness.

Conclusions

The model of mentoring that we describe in this chapter is a promising framework for understanding conditions that lead to beneficial outcomes in youth mentoring programs. Fundamentally, it emphasizes that youth should come to view their mentors as significant persons and sources of support in their lives. It is therefore important to ask: What can be done to enhance the likelihood that this occurs? Clearly, agencies should make efforts to strengthen features of programs with this goal in mind. Few, if any, existing programs have implemented the entire range of identified best practices (see Table 2.1). The Big Brothers Big Sisters affiliate that we examined, for example, did not incorporate agency-sponsored activities to promote mentor-youth interaction, a component facilitating communication between mentors and parents, or ongoing (or postmatch) training for mentors. Program-level innovations may help to ensure that mentors are in a position to provide a broad range of support functions to youth. Program developers should place a premium on fostering those types of assistance likely to enhance the personal resources and strengths of youth.[23] Our results call particular attention to the value of helping mentors to promote healthy and positive self-esteem.

Program-level initiatives must be complemented, however, by efforts to monitor and support the development of individual relationships.[32] Programs should work closely with each pairing of mentor and youth to help ensure the success of that relationship. The challenges and unique qualities inherent in any mentoring relationship, coupled with findings indicating the importance of relationship characteristics for predicting outcomes, underscore the importance of this conclusion. In the meta-analysis of mentoring program effectiveness, the poorest outcomes were found for youth exhibiting individual-level risk factors or vulnerabilities.[7] Programs will have to make more in-depth or intensive efforts to facilitate positive relationships for this subgroup.

Needs for future research parallel the preceding concerns. There is a need for increased understanding of factors contributing to mentoring effectiveness at the levels of both program characteristics and individual relationships within programs. Furthermore, models of relationship development are needed that delineate desirable patterns of change or growth in mentor-youth interactions and experiences over time. To meet these goals, studies will need to include multiple programs as well as detailed longitudinal examination of individual relationships within them. The present study, for example, included only a single Big Brothers Big Sisters affiliate and thus was inherently limited in its ability to investigate program-level influences. To date, the types of multiprogram studies needed to address this concern have been a rarity in the mentoring literature. In our view, they should receive much higher priority in the future.

Mentoring programs are an important component of efforts to promote positive youth development. It is essential, however, that programs be designed and implemented in ways that are effective. A guiding focus should be the understanding that, ultimately, beneficial outcomes will be dependent on the relationships formed between individual mentors and youth. Programs should be oriented to ensuring, at a minimum, that participating youth come to perceive and experience their mentors as significant adults in their lives. The model presented and tested in this chapter is a promising first step in delineating specific processes through which strong mentoring relationships can be beneficial for youth.

Notes

1. Offord, D. R. (1995). Child psychiatric epidemiology: Current status and future prospects. *Canadian Journal of Psychiatry, 40,* 284–288.

2. Mash, E. J., & Dozois, D. J. (1997). Child psychopathology: A developmental-systems perspective. In E. J. Mash & R. A. Barkley (Eds.), *Child psychopathology* (pp. 3–60). New York: Guilford Press.

3. Durlak, J. A., & Wells, A. M. (1997). Primary prevention mental health programs for children and adolescents. *American Journal of Community Psychology, 25,* 115–152.

4. Rhodes, J. E. (in press). *Stand by me: Risks and rewards in youth mentoring.* Cambridge, MA: Harvard University Press.

5. Johnson, A. W., & Sullivan, J. W. (1995). Mentoring program practices and effectiveness. In M. Galbraith & N. Cohen (Eds.), *Mentoring: New strategies and challenges* (pp. 43–56). San Francisco: Jossey-Bass.

6. Rhodes, J. E. (1994). Older and wiser: Mentoring relationships in childhood and adolescence. *Journal of Primary Prevention, 14,* 187–196.

7. DuBois, D. L., Holloway, B. E., Valentine, J. C., & Cooper, H. (in press). Effectiveness of mentoring programs for youth: A meta-analytic review. *American Journal of Community Psychology.*

8. National Mentoring Working Group. (1991). *Mentoring: Elements of effective practice.* Washington, DC: National Mentoring Partnership.

9. Huisman, C. (1992). *Student mentoring program 1989–1992: Evaluation report.* Portland: Oregon Community Foundation.

10. LoSciuto, L., Rajala, A. K., Townsend, T. N., & Taylor, A. S. (1996). An outcome evaluation of Across Ages: An intergenerational mentoring approach to drug prevention. *Journal of Adolescent Research, 11,* 116–129.

11. Dicken, C., Bryson, R., & Kass, N. (1977). Companionship therapy: A replication of experimental community psychology. *Journal of Consulting and Clinical Psychology, 4,* 637–642.

12. Slicker, E. K., & Palmer, D. J. (1993). Mentoring at-risk high school students: Evaluation of a school-based program. *School Counselor, 40,* 327–333.

13. Royse, D. (1998). Mentoring high-risk minority youth: Evaluation of the Brothers project. *Adolescence, 33,* 145–158.

14. Howitt, P. S., Moore, E. A., & Gaulier, B. (1998). Winning the battles and the wars: An evaluation of comprehensive, community-based delinquency prevention programming. *Juvenile and Family Court Journal, 49,* 39–49.

15. Lambert, M. J., Shapiro, D. A., & Bergin, A. E. (1986). The effectiveness of psychotherapy. In S. L. Garfield & A. E. Bergin (Eds.), *Handbook of psychotherapy and behavior change* (3d ed., pp. 157–211). New York: Wiley.

16. Cauce, A. M., Coronado, N., & Watson, J. (1998). Conceptual, methodological, and statistical issues in culturally competent research. In M. Hernandez & R. Mareasa (Eds.), *Promoting cultural competence in children's mental health service: Systems of care for children's mental health* (pp. 305–329). Baltimore: Brookes Publishing.

17. Grossman, J. B., & Rhodes, J. E. (in press). The test of time: Predictors and effects of duration in youth mentoring programs. *American Journal of Community Psychology.*

18. Stanwyck, D. A., & Anson, C. A. (1989). *The Adopt-a-Student evaluation project: Final report.* Atlanta: Georgia State University, Department of Educational Foundations.

19. Johnson, A. W. (1997). Mentoring at-risk youth: A research review and

evaluation of the impacts of the Sponsor-A-Scholar Program on student performance. Unpublished doctoral dissertation, University of Pennsylvania, 1997. Abstract in *Dissertation Abstracts International, 58*(3), 813A.

20. Rhodes, J. E., Contreras, J. M., & Mangelsdorf, S. C. (1994). Natural mentor relationships among Latina adolescent mothers: Psychological adjustment, moderating processes, and the role of early parental acceptance. *American Journal of Community Psychology, 22,* 211–227.

21. Rhodes, J. E., Ebert, L., & Fischer, K. (1992). Natural mentors: An overlooked resource in the social networks of African-American adolescent mothers. *American Journal of Community Psychology, 20,* 445–462.

22. Hirsch, B. J., Roffman, J. G., Pagano, M. E., & Deutsch, N. L. (2000, April). Inner city youth: Ties to youth development staff and adult kin. In B. Sanchez (Chair), *Natural and volunteer mentoring relationships of adolescents.* Symposium conducted at the biennial meeting of the Society for Research on Adolescence, Chicago.

23. Sandler, I. N. (2001). The intersection of, and interaction between, theory development and practice in prevention science. *American Journal of Community Psychology, 29,* 17–61.

24. DuBois, D. L., & Tevendale, H. D. (1999). Self-esteem in childhood and adolescence: Vaccine or epiphenomenon? *Applied and Preventive Psychology, 8,* 103–117.

25. Rhodes, J. E., Grossman, J. B., & Resch, N. L. (2000). Agents of change: Pathways through which mentoring relationships influence adolescents' academic adjustment. *Child Development, 71,* 1662–1671.

26. Petersen, A. C., Kennedy, R. E., & Sullivan, P. A. (1991). Coping with adolescence. In M. E. Colten & S. Gore (Eds.), *Adolescent stress: Causes and consequences* (pp. 93–110). Hawthorne, NY: Aldine De Gruyter.

27. Sandler, I. N., & Twohey, J. L. (1998). Conceptualization and measurement of coping in children and adolescents. *Advances in Clinical Child Psychology, 20,* 243–301.

28. Grossman, J. B., & Tierney, J. P. (1998). Does mentoring work? An impact study of the Big Brothers Big Sisters program. *Evaluation Review, 22,* 403–426.

29. Blakely, C. H., Menon, R., & Jones, D. C. (1995). *Project BELONG: Final report.* College Station: Public Policy Research Institute, Texas A&M University.

30. Freedman, M. (1988). *Partners in growth: Elder mentors and at-risk youth.* Philadelphia: Public/Private Ventures.

31. Herrera, C., Sipe, C. L., & McClanahan, W. S. (2000). *Making mentoring relationships better: Program, matching and activity factors that contribute to mentors' positive relationships with youth.* Philadelphia: Public/Private Ventures.

32. Parra, G. R., DuBois, D. L., Neville, H. A., & Pugh, A. O. (2001). *Mentoring relationships for youth: Predictors of perceived benefits and longevity.* Manuscript submitted for publication.

33. Tierney, J. P., Grossman, J. B., & Resch, N. L. (1995). *Making a difference: An impact study of Big Brothers/Big Sisters.* Philadelphia: Public/Private Ventures.

34. Bandura, A. (1995). *Self-efficacy in changing societies.* Cambridge: Cambridge University Press.

35. Achenbach, T. M. (1991). *Integrative guide for the 1991 CBCL/4–18, YSR, and TRF profiles*. Burlington: University of Vermont Department of Psychiatry.

36. Procidano, M. E., & Heller, K. (1983). Measures of perceived social support from friends and from family: Three validation studies. *American Journal of Community Psychology, 11*, 1–24.

37. DuBois, D. L., et al. (1996). Early adolescent self-esteem: A developmental-ecological framework and assessment strategy. *Journal of Research on Adolescence, 6*, 543–579.

38. DuBois, D. L., et al. (2000). *Getting by with a little help from self and others: Self-esteem and social support as resources during early adolescence*. Manuscript submitted for publication.

39. Causey, D. L., & Dubow, E. F. (1992). Development of a self-report coping measure for elementary school children. *Journal of Clinical Child Psychology, 21*, 47–59.

40. Sayer, A. G. (1998, February). *Advances in methods for analyzing longitudinal data*. Paper presented at the seventh biennial meeting of the Society for Research on Adolescence, San Diego, CA.

41. Bentler, P. M. (1996). EQS: A structural equations program, Version 5.1. Multivariate Software, Inc., Encino, Calif.

42. MacCallum, R. C. (1995). Model specification: Procedures, strategies, and related issues. In R. H. Hoyle (Ed.), *Structural equation modeling: Concepts, issues, and applications* (pp. 16–36). Thousand Oaks, CA: Sage.

43. Taylor, R. (1996). Adolescents' perceptions of kinship support and family management practices: Association with adolescent adjustment in African American families. *Developmental Psychology, 32*, 687–695.

44. DuBois, D. L., Felner, R. D., Brand, S., & George, G. R. (1999). Profiles of self-esteem in early adolescence: Identification and investigation of adaptive correlates. *American Journal of Community Psychology, 27*, 899–932.

DAVID L. DUBOIS *is associate professor of psychology at the University of Missouri, Columbia.*

HELEN A. NEVILLE *is assistant professor at the University of California, Santa Barbara.*

GILBERT R. PARRA *is a graduate student in the clinical psychology program at the University of Missouri, Columbia.*

AALECE O. PUGH-LILLY *is assistant professor of counseling psychology at Teacher's College, University of Nebraska.*

Workplaces are ideal contexts for mentoring rela-
tionships between adults and older youth. To teach
the competencies required in contemporary work-
places (many of which are equally useful in other
settings), mentors need to use sophisticated teaching
behaviors, which the authors characterize as reflec-
tive questioning and problem solving.

3

Why mentoring in the workplace works

Mary Agnes Hamilton, Stephen F. Hamilton

GIVEN THE RIGHT conditions, youth in all cultures across time have
strived to learn how to do good work, to participate in social organizations, and to act responsibly. Yet as early as 1928, Margaret
Mead acknowledged that many psychologists and parents perceived
adolescence as a period of turbulence.[1] In an effort to understand
whether this *"Sturm und Drang"* were endemic to their developmental age or to their culture, she traveled to Samoa to observe
adolescent girls in their daily life as part of a family and community and to see how their experiences prepared them for adulthood.

Mead described striking differences between the United States
and Samoa. For example, Samoan children and adolescents learned
to care for all in their society; they made fewer choices than American youth; and Samoan children did not play at adult work tasks.
"From the time they are four or five years old they perform definite tasks, . . . which have a meaning in the structure of the whole
society. . . . Work consists of those necessary tasks which keep the
social life going: planting and harvesting and preparation of food,

NEW DIRECTIONS FOR YOUTH DEVELOPMENT, NO. 93, SPRING 2002 © WILEY PERIODICALS, INC.

fishing, house-building, mat-making, care of children, collecting of property to validate marriages and births and succession to titles and to entertain strangers, these are the necessary activities of life, activities in which every member of the community, down to the smallest child, has a part." What was particularly revolutionary for her time and prescient of ours was the conclusion that storm and stress are not inherent in adolescence, that adolescents could experience a less stressful maturation process under different cultural conditions: "adolescence is not necessarily a time of stress and strain, but . . . cultural conditions make it so."

Mead suggested that to function effectively in our society adults need to achieve a higher level of thinking and skill development than in Samoa. "The principal causes of our adolescents' difficulty are the presence of conflicting standards and the belief that every individual should make his or her own choices, coupled with a feeling that choice is an important matter." Similarities between Samoan society, with fewer choices, more consistent expectations, and fewer requirements for advanced knowledge and skill, can be seen historically in the United States. Public schools, created initially during the industrial age to enable citizens to read newspapers and the Bible and to write letters and do simple arithmetic, expanded to provide more advanced education to a much larger segment of the population as workers moved from farms into factories and offices. And as the industrial age is succeeded by the information age, the kind of challenging education once limited to students preparing for the elite professions is now needed by the masses.

The labor market has clearly signaled employers' preference for workers with more educational credentials: the gap in employment between workers with only a high school diploma and those with a college degree has increased substantially over the past twenty-five years as information processing and other services have grown and manufacturing has receded.[2] The daunting and perplexing goal facing public schools in the United States and other postindustrial nations is to educate masses of youth to levels formerly achieved by only a small minority. Schools have the institutional responsibility to increase youth's capacity to master more challenging learning to make informed choices as citizens and family members as well as workers, a charge parallel to that articulated by Mead in the early twentieth century. "Adaptive learning" includes not only basic facts and routine skills but also how to think critically, how to solve problems, how to analyze data and ideas, how to work cooperatively as well as independently, how to communicate using a variety of media, how to continue learning for a lifetime, and how to make commitments to values and make lifestyle choices from among a multitude of competing possibilities.[3]

Extending school enrollment for all is clearly one response to this goal, but it is just as clearly inadequate in itself. We learned in the second half of the twentieth century that being in school is not the same as getting a good education. Raising standards for all is another response: students must be expected to learn more and to learn more deeply than in the past. But these responses are constrained by existing academic structures and conventional assumptions about what young people need to learn and how they learn. The learning needs of citizens in an information age are not limited to academics, nor can these needs be met solely in schools. The ability to work cooperatively and to take initiative, to name two such needs, are not the fruits of book learning.

The most thorough and influential treatment of nonacademic learning needs comes from the Secretary of Labor's Commission on Achieving Necessary Skills,[4] which identified a set of both academic and nonacademic learning objectives that are now referred to as "the SCANS skills." A few years later, Murnane and Levy demonstrated the value of nonacademic "soft skills,"[2] finding that these skills, rather than differences in academic knowledge, distinguished factory workers who were promoted from those who were not.

Domains of competence

With this as our background, we began looking at ways in which modern youth are learning the nonacademic skills needed in a postindustrial society. Working with employers and educators to identify learning goals for a particular youth apprenticeship demonstration project, we found it helpful to use the term *competence* to incorporate both knowledge and skill and to distinguish three domains of competence: technical, personal, and social. *Technical competence* is revealed in the performance of tasks, doing the job right. *Personal competence* refers to individual qualities related to acting responsibly, drawing on self-confidence, initiative (drive), and career planning. *Social competence* refers to the capacity to work with others and participate in an organization, and it includes rules, teamwork, and communication. Adopting this framework for thinking about what young people need to learn leads quickly to recognition that the competencies employers desire are needed as well by active citizens in a democracy and by nurturing family members. They serve, that is to say, as a way of defining broad domains of adolescent development.

Moreover, the framework is equally applicable to preindustrial societies,[5] now or in earlier historical periods. Young people growing up as subsistence farmers need to acquire technical competence, often strictly gender-related, to cultivate the soil, tend animals, build and maintain houses and barns, and harvest, store, and prepare food. Personal competence remains essential, although its definition is different in such conditions, which typically call for an identity that is less individual and more collective. (For example, initiative is likely to be required less than deference to authority.) And social competence is also different but still necessary. It entails performing a well-defined role in a small, close-knit group that shares common values. Communication is less challenging because language and culture are more homogeneous. However, interactions with others outside the group may demand complex negotiating skills and the capacity to understand and respond to very different people, including representatives of a national government or a global corporation, entities that intrude more and more into previously isolated areas.

Settings in which competencies are attained

Noting the nature of the technical, personal, and social competencies youth learn in preindustrial societies underlines an important point about learning in information-age societies: these competencies are not learned only in schools. Schools do effectively and efficiently teach academic disciplines, one aspect of technical competence. (It would be naive to expect a hospital lab to assume responsibility to teach high school interns biology or organic chemistry.) However, we believe schools are less than optimal environments for acquiring many employment-related competencies and even for fostering adaptive learning of conventional academic subjects. Among the weaknesses of school learning are its divorce from application and its atomization into discrete subjects. Students can learn to answer test questions correctly yet be stumped by the simplest real-world problems that require combining and applying knowledge.

As cognitive scientists have extended their investigations into how people learn the kinds of things they use in their daily lives—as distinct from the kinds of things they learn in school—they have investigated teaching and learning in preindustrial societies where imitation and gradual induction into adult activities predominate over formal schooling or even conscious instruction.[6] Schlegel and Barry reviewed ethnographic studies of adolescence in 186 preindustrial societies, reporting that "few ethnographies discuss work of adolescents, simply indicating that adolescent boys work alongside their fathers and girls alongside their mothers, unless boys have some specialized task like herding cattle."[7] Lave and Wenger coined the term *legitimate peripheral participation* to describe this mode of learning. Apprenticeship is its epitome.[8] We have been especially interested in the fact that learning in an apprenticeship setting is embedded in a social relationship between an adolescent and an adult who is neither a schoolteacher nor a parent but rather a mentor.

The idea of mentoring is firmly rooted in the commonsense belief that it is good for a young person to have a close relationship with a caring older person, other than a parent, who can teach and advise and simply be an adult in her or his presence. In preindustrial societies, where most people are deeply involved in producing the necessities of life, such relationships can form naturally, in the course of daily life. Industrialization sharply separated work life from family life, workplaces from neighborhoods, and adults from youth. Schools round up all the youth in the community and segregate them with each other and a few teachers; then adults complain about peer pressure and ask why the youth don't grow up. One reason mentoring programs are so popular now is that we recognize the need to bridge the gap we have created between young people and adults outside the school and family. Well-designed mentoring programs have demonstrated impressive power to improve the lives of young people.[9]

In addition to closing the gap between young people and adults, mentoring can help to bridge some of the gaps created between people because of differences in income, education, and race. Mentors reach out to young people who are different from themselves and help them set and meet their own goals. In addition, mentoring can assume different forms for different situations. For example, our research and program development on mentoring more than ten years ago convinced us that the social mentoring approach exemplified by Big Brothers Big Sisters, effective as it is for elementary- and middle-school-age children, is not well suited to high-school-age youth.[10] Children and early adolescents get excited about the chance to go places and do things with an older person. However, as they gain mobility and independence and become more involved in activities with peers, older adolescents no longer find social mentoring appealing. In the program we evaluated, many adult-youth pairs never got to the first stage of simply meeting regularly. Those that did tended to meet to accomplish something together, not just to talk or have fun.

On the other hand, doing "real" things is very appealing, and work is real. According to the National Research Council, "about 80 percent of teens work at some time during the school year in their junior or senior years in high school."[11] Even young people who are employed in what most adults would consider dull, routine work often find the experience satisfying: doing something important, learning things that others cannot do, and being in the company of adults and treated like peers—not to mention earning money, our society's ultimate criterion of value.

The work ethic is so central to our culture that questioning the value of work experience for youth development seems obtuse.

However, since the pathbreaking research of Greenberger and Steinberg,[12] many studies have demonstrated that working long hours while enrolled in high school is associated with such undesirable characteristics as higher absenteeism and reduced educational aspirations; more lying, aggressive behavior, and minor delinquency; and greater use of tobacco, alcohol, and illegal drugs. On the other hand, working while in high school is also associated with higher levels of employment and earnings after graduation. According to the authoritative review of research on high school students' employment in *Protecting Youth at Work*, high-intensity work (defined both by hours per week and number of weeks per school year) is most detrimental,[11] whereas other studies show low-intensity work to have mostly positive effects, including increased college enrollment.[13] Although there is no evidence of a sharp cut-off point, investigators generally define twenty hours of work per week or more as intensive or excessive, less for younger workers. Although few studies provide sufficient detail about the nature of youth work experience to allow careful differentiation, such qualities as being able to acquire and use skills, seeing a relation between the job and one's future, and making connections between school and work all seem to enhance positive effects and reduce negative effects. The evidence is strong enough to compel attention to the nature and quality of the work experience, in addition to its presence, absence, and intensity.

Workplaces can be good environments for the development of mentoring relationships. Mentoring youth at work, the topic of this chapter, is different from corporate mentoring, in which corporations encourage their employees to become mentors for youth outside the workplace.[14] One advantage of putting youth together with adults in workplaces is that the focus is on learning to do a job. Sometimes it is precisely this attention to completing a task that sets the stage for a relationship that goes beyond getting the job done. Good work-based learning incorporates mentoring: adults teach youth not only how to do the work but how to behave as adult workers, and some of those adults become confidants or advisers. In some workplaces, youth are matched with a single mentor for their entire stay; in others, they might rotate through multiple placements and therefore work with multiple mentors.

A mentor is an older, more experienced person who seeks to further the development of character and competence in a younger person by guiding the latter in acquiring mastery of progressively more complex skills and tasks in which the mentor is already proficient. The guidance is accomplished through demonstration, instruction, challenge, and encouragement on a more or less regular basis over an extended period of time. In the course of this process, the mentor and the young person develop a special bond of mutual commitment. In addition, the young person's relationship to the mentor takes on an emotional character of respect, loyalty, and identification.[15]

The study

Sample and procedures

The findings presented in this chapter come from interviews with forty-two mentors and twenty-six of their protégés from our study, Mentoring Youth at Work, which was designed to test a conceptual framework about how and what mentors teach youth in workplaces.[16] We used findings from an initial set of interviews with highly recommended experienced mentors as a basis for a training program for novice mentors. For the next phase of the study, we selected work-based learning programs in eight communities that acknowledged technical, social, and personal learning as a primary purpose and where one or more adults had the responsibility to supervise the learning of each youth. In addition, we sought programs that involved at least two hundred hours of work experience (although some programs proved to be less intensive). The mentors considered youth to be apprentices, interns, students, or employees. They were placed in workplaces matching their career interests.

We paired the communities geographically, then selected one in each pair by coin toss to receive the mentor training program. We interviewed mentors in both communities up to four times over a six-month period; youth were interviewed once. Results were used to validate and refine the training program. Interviewers asked mentors to generate a list of the most important things they tried to teach their protégés and then to describe situations when they tried to teach those things. Youth were asked equivalent questions to generate a list and follow-up questions for each item on the list: "I'd like you to tell me the most important things you got out of your [internship, apprenticeship, job, and so on]"; "Tell me about a situation when your mentor helped you with learning [first item on youth's list]." The purpose of the interviews was to explore the impact of the training on what mentors taught and how they taught it. Here, we report findings only from control mentors who did not have our training, because we wish to understand what mentors do without training in how to teach. Some programs offered orientation to mentors, but none trained them in teaching methods.

Despite our efforts to limit the sample to novice mentors, 52 percent of the control group had more than a year of experience (as did 50 percent of the treatment group). The control mentors worked in a range of occupations, with 45 percent in manufacturing and engineering technology and the trades, 29 percent in the business field, and representation in the arts and media, education and social services, and health care. Case material that illustrates the learning goals and teaching behaviors is taken from the broader mentoring study, which included interviews with expert mentors, and from a previous study of youth apprenticeship as well. Many of the stories are incorporated into mentor training materials and are available on our Web site, http://www.human.cornell.edu/youthwork/.

What mentors teach and how

Control mentors described teaching youth by explaining how and why and by monitoring. Only one person did not explicitly talk about teaching by demonstrating. We categorized these four teaching behaviors as universal because virtually all mentors in the control group said they had used them at one time or other in their interviews. Stasz and Kaganoff, observing youth in work-based learning programs, also found a predominance of universal teaching behaviors, which they labeled "show and tell."[17] (However, they did not distinguish explaining how from explaining why or report on monitoring.)

Less frequent in the mentor stories are questioning and problem solving: 67 percent said they had used questioning, whereas 41 percent had used problem solving. These behaviors challenge youth to think and analyze problems, and they are more challenging for mentors to use as well. For both of these reasons, we categorized questioning and problem solving as challenging teaching behaviors. Our interviews were designed to elicit mentors' and youths' descriptions of teaching behavior in the three competence domains: technical, personal, and social (without imposing any of these categories). We view challenging workplace teaching as a critical contribution to helping young people master the high level of technical, personal, and social competencies demanded by contemporary workplaces and by their roles as citizens and family members in the twenty-first century. This is especially true for young people who do not acquire these competencies at home or in school.

Teaching youth how to do the job right

Technical competence

Technical competence includes not only mastering procedures but also understanding fundamental principles and concepts underlying procedures, increasing capacity for analytical judgment, and becoming computer literate. Learning at work should give youth a firm foundation of knowledge and skills that includes the concepts and principles anchored in the related academic disciplines, appreciation for expertise, confidence in their own ability, and the understanding that learning continues for a lifetime. Learning to perform a job task, the fundamental technical competence, is the competency our control mentors report most frequently that they teach

(100 percent). Other technical competencies reported include meeting productivity standards (48 percent), organizing work tasks (33 percent), and meeting safety standards (41 percent).

The control mentors described teaching their protégés how to do job tasks by demonstrating (86 percent), explaining how to do it (98 percent), explaining why to do it a certain way (93 percent), and monitoring their progress (100 percent), that is, observing their performance and giving feedback about it. Recall that we call these four teaching behaviors universal because, as illustrated by the percentages just reported for teaching how to perform job tasks, almost all mentors reported using them when asked how they taught.

Strikingly fewer control mentors mentioned that they had used reflective questioning (50 percent) or problem solving (36 percent)—the so-called challenging teaching behaviors—to teach how to perform job tasks. Moreover, these percentages include indication during any of the repeated interviews that a mentor used such behaviors. For any single round of interviews, the highest rate for reflective questioning was 23 percent of mentors and for problem solving 26 percent.

One youth in a manufacturing firm explained how a mentor helped him internalize the value of quality work.

The most important thing I've learned from my mentor is that it looks easy when he tells it to you and when you have it on paper, but when you start working on it it's not as easy as it seems. Like when we did this block, he gave me a block of wood, a rectangle shape, and he said, "We need to fit four screws on the top and three screws on the bottom." I said, "Okay, this is going to be real easy. All you got to do is take the screw and put a dot." And so then, I didn't drill it or anything. I just took the blocks and the screws, plotted it. And then I marked the holes and I showed it to my mentor and I said, "Here you go. I'm done. Ten minutes." And he said, "Is that it?" And I said, "Yes." He asked me if I was really done with it, and then he drew it on the chalkboard, and he explained that the way I did it, just plotting it on there, would not work. It would come out all crooked. And then he showed me how you take measurements from each dimension with the screws and how you plot it on there the correct way, taking measurements and taking into account the size of the hole and the size of the screw. That project really opened my eyes to what they do on the floor in actuality. When you do work, you do quality work. You try to meet and exceed the customers' expectations. You try to do top-of-the-line quality work because not only is the company's work top-of-the-line, you're also putting your name onto that project that you're doing. So you want to do the best work that you can and put a lot of effort and quality into it.

This youth's account illustrates how a mentor taught by assigning a project or a problem to solve and then working with the youth to get it done right. One can infer that the experience was more powerful than it would have been if the mentor had simply demonstrated or explained how to locate the screws correctly.

Involvement in long-term projects that entail planning and carrying out multiple steps introduces youth to all aspects of the industry rather than merely teaching them to perform a single job. By their nature, such projects engage youth in aspects of work beyond their daily assignments; they often require teamwork as well. They foster deeper understanding of multiple workplace issues. Opportunities to engage in such projects vary widely. Some workplaces, such as insurance company back offices, are organized around routine and repetition. In others, such as electrical contractors, each job is a new project, requiring planning and the mastery of new tasks. A mentor who is a dentist described how she helped her summer intern take responsibility for planning the clinic's part in a health fair for children.

As a summer intern in our pediatric dental clinic, Sarah planned a dental health station at a Head Start health fair. Ours was one of about nine different stations at the fair, which lasted three days. One was vision, another hearing. I was asked to plan the dental aspect of it. I turned the planning over to her. She was also responsible for making arrangements. It was a big thing for her because she had to put together all of the components. She had to call up the health coordinator at Head Start and introduce herself to this woman. The woman is very busy, so she had to catch up with her first of all. Then she had to tell her that she had been assigned the dental part. I explained to her how I had done it because I had done it the year before. I told her to talk to the woman to find out what the woman wanted. So she used me as a resource. I didn't dictate to her. She planned it, and she gave me a role. She had to find out from the woman in charge where our station for the mobile van was going to be. She had to make a sign. She had to call up the doctors. She had to get the volunteers. She had to make cold calls. It would be unpredictable how many people would be in line, so she had to figure out what to do with the people who are waiting. She figured out that this would be a good time to provide some dental health education to them. She also needed to fill out the consent forms. And she needed to record who came. She figured out she couldn't do everything, so my dental assistant needed to help out. I needed to help out. There were a few days when I couldn't do it, so she knew she needed to find somebody else. She needed to plan for the worst scenario, which is that conceivably all eight hundred children could show up on the first day. So she had two dentists for each day. And we had toothbrushes and toothpaste.

This project, which also illustrates the teaching behavior we call problem solving, reveals both the collaborative nature of the process and the impressive levels of independence and responsibility that high school interns can achieve under the right circumstances.

Teaching youth to get along at the workplace

Personal and social competence

Employers frequently say that the qualifications they value most in entry-level employees are not technical skills but such traits as punctuality, reliability, and diligence—personal and social competence, in our terms. Employers claim that people who have demonstrated personal and social competence can be trained in technical skills. In other words, it is easier to teach people how to perform work tasks than how to be good workers. Gaining personal and social competence is critical for youth, therefore, because such competence endures and is needed in any workplace, whereas many technical competencies are site specific and are outmoded as new technologies are introduced. Moreover, the same personal and social competencies that employers seek are applicable outside the workplace in young people's lives as citizens and family members.

Teaching youth how to act responsibly

Personal competence

Adults focus on teaching personal competence by providing opportunities for youth to take initiative and to take responsibility for continued learning, to gain self-confidence, and to plan for their careers. Indicators of youth learning to act responsibly include taking initiative when appropriate, asking questions and seeking help in a timely fashion, performing tasks with measured assurance, having the courage to ask for help, seeking counsel about career options and pathways, and pursuing rigorous academic courses to qualify for further education.

Drive. We categorized as *drive* mentors' goals such as teaching youth to take initiative, to suggest improvements, and to take responsibility for continued learning. After performing job tasks, drive is the teaching goal that control mentors most frequently named. Ninety-one percent of them talked about using universal teaching behaviors to teach youth about drive. But again, only 14 percent talked about using challenging behaviors to meet this goal. A mentor in a high-tech electronics firm described how he encouraged a youth to assume a high degree of accountability for his work, another aspect of drive. "I might come back and say to him, 'Remember, we talked about that image that has a watermark on it, and you need to get the one that doesn't have a watermark on it? Have you done that?' So he kind of learns that he's got a lot of latitude and a lot of responsibility, but there is at some point some accountability somewhere."

The mentor went on to describe how he might engage the youth in diagnosing a problem: "So what's your version, or what's your view of this?" We classify these teaching behaviors as monitoring and reflective questioning, because the mentor is following up to see whether a lesson has been learned and posing a question designed to encourage the youth's thinking. The mentor went on to say that eventually the intern would "proactively raise a question about something that looks like it's not getting finished on time. And it's not just that he wanted to preempt my questioning; it's that he's internalized the value of keeping on top of things, [something] which he did not have before. . . . So there's some sense in there that we're talking about the integrity of human interactions, not just getting the job done, I think. . . . I hope."

Self-confidence. Half of the control mentors (52 percent) worked on building their protégés' self-confidence. Only two mentioned a challenging teaching behavior. The following mentor described how he explained to his protégé that his lack of confidence was interfering with his job performance.

The first thing I start with is confidence. They absolutely have to believe in themselves. You're dealing with young people. They're coming in to work with a stranger. I remember what it was like to be a young guy. I didn't have a lot of confidence when I was a young guy. The first young man I worked with, he came in and he was very, very shy and very quiet, very reserved, very nervous. It was getting to the point where he was so afraid of doing anything that he was making a lot of mistakes because he was worried all the time. We actually had to sit down and talk one day, and I had to tell him point blank, "This is about you. This isn't about me or anybody else here." I said, "This is about you, and it appears to me that you don't feel at times that you're equal to anybody here." And I told him, "You need to get over that, because you are no better and you are no worse than anybody else that is here. And until you believe that, it's going to continue affecting how you do your job." And he got it. It changed.

This was an unusual example because the mentor discussed the need for self-confidence explicitly. Mentors are more likely to say they boost their protégés' self-confidence by giving them praise.

Career planning. A career path traces a lifelong occupational journey involving both education and employment, not a single job or even a single occupation. By this definition, some career paths are smooth and direct, whereas others are rough and full of dead ends; some lead to well-paid and prestigious employment, but others do not. A path is not a track; it allows for changes in direction and can lead toward several destinations. No one has ever been able to predict precisely where his or her own career path or someone else's will lead, and detailed certainty about the future is now inconceivable. But young people can make better choices if they can get a better sense of what they can do in the future and what they have to do to prepare.

Having a career path in mind provides a sense of direction and motivates academic achievement so that a young person is well prepared even if she or he later chooses a different path. High school seniors without a vision of a career path often see no reason to take math or science courses that are not required. A student who takes an extra science course because she wants to become a physical therapy assistant not only prepares for that career goal but also preserves the option of continuing her studies to become an actual physical therapist or even a physician, options foreclosed or at least made less easily attainable if she takes only the minimum requirements. Although 74 percent of the control mentors said they taught their protégés about career paths, only 24 percent used challenging teaching behaviors for this purpose, as illustrated by a banker.

She just doesn't know if she sees a need for college. And I really—we think she should. And she's got the grades to do it. We've talked about it quite a few times, on down times. I'll say, "Okay, what do you think your plans are? You're a junior, you've got to start." And she'll say, "Yes, yes, I've been looking at this, but I don't like that." And then we had this big long discussion. I had the bank's vice president join the discussion, and I think just having men involved with the conversation too just really—I think she's really thinking about it now. And with this youth, we've got to try and get her motivated. I talk about my son in college a lot with her. And she does think that's pretty neat, you know, what his goals are in life. I guess maybe just relating, and she knows my son.

When we interviewed this banker's protégé, she recounted how her mentor had opened new opportunities and choices for her that she had not foreseen before working at the bank.

Yeah, we talk about that [future plans] all the time; she gives me suggestions on colleges and different areas of the bank that I could go to and things like that, the different things that I could possibly do in the future, and stuff I could go to school for. She's told me many times that there's so many different areas of banking that you can get into and that there's not just the teller stuff, that you can go really high up in the business if you really want to and that there are a lot of colleges that have good finance programs. When I first started working as a teller, I'm like, "Is this all I'm going to be doing?" By her showing me all the different areas and telling me, it made me realize that this is really something that I could do, because you could go from area to area, and you could move up so much. You don't have to just stay in one spot. She doesn't really know what classes are required for certain areas. She's just told me that the accounting classes are real good to take. If you have a background in accounting, it looks real good, like on a résumé when you go to any position.

Teaching youth how to participate in an organization

Social competence

Social qualities such as the ability to communicate, to work effectively with diverse groups of people, and to be trustworthy and honest are fundamental goals of youth development. When youth make the transition to full-time employment, these competencies allow them to work in teams and adhere to professional norms, to navigate organizational systems, and to give clear messages to people within them.

Rules. The subcategory of social competence most frequently mentioned by the control mentors was rules and norms. Eighty-three percent talked at some point about teaching youth to adhere to the rules and norms of the workplace. Only 12 percent described using challenging teaching behaviors for this purpose. A mentor in an engineering firm described how he challenged his protégé to build self-discipline and personal integrity.

One of the things I saw that Jerome was somewhat slack on was discipline. When I would set up a meeting with him, he thought it was okay to show up late. I know one time for sure he showed up late to a meeting, and I couldn't meet with him. I told him he had lost his slot. I told him, "We have a time schedule, and you weren't there." And I said, "Not only were you not there, you didn't call me." I think that was the last time he was late. And I'm hoping that carries over into school, into the next job he might have. There were a few times when I would proofread and then I would make corrections. He brought me the copy the next week, and I noticed some of the corrections I had given him had not been made. And we got into a discussion about why he was wasting my time. I [like to] put [an issue] on the table and deal with it, OK? Because I think if I allow him to get away with it here, he might have felt going to college he could slip, slide, and skate, or do what I call a Peggy Fleming—try to skate through. And I felt that I needed to be firm with him but at the same time be fair. For the most part, I think he appreciated it.

Systems. Social competence includes learning about work organizations as systems, including such aspects as purposes, structure, the connections between departments and other units, the roles of people in the organization, obligations to clients and customers, and how to gain access to information. When work tasks and projects provide insights into how the firm operates, young people can understand how their work contributes to the firm as a whole, and they become more enthusiastic and more productive. Fifty-two percent of the control mentors mentioned that they used universal teaching behaviors related to systems; only one talked about using challenging teaching behavior for this purpose.

One mentor used a youth's request for an immediate change in his work placement as an opportunity to teach him how an organization works and reassess his approach to the problem.

Ron came to me at the point where he wanted to be moved to another department or he was going to quit. He was in that all-or-nothing mode. He wanted to just basically go tell the manager, "You have to move me out of this department." I calmly explained to him that if he went about it in a more diplomatic manner, if he just explained without yelling at his manager that he was not in the position that he desired, that he would have a better chance of being moved out. I helped him to understand that you just can't give a manager an ultimatum unless you are ready to walk out the door yourself. Because that's what happens in a corporate world. If you give a manager an ultimatum that says, "Move me or [I'll] quit," it's "Hey, clean your desk out." He explained that he did not want to do just this side of the business. And he was also disappointed because he wanted to get back into other facets of the business. He said, "I know I don't want to do this. Why are they making me do it?" I said, "Well, explain it to them. Don't be upset. Explain it to them that you want to learn these other fields, but don't come off that 'I'm not going to do that anymore or I'm going to quit.' If you go up and start demanding something from somebody or crying out unnecessarily, you might find yourself in a position that you'll need this person's services later. If you go about it in a professional manner and you ask them in a courteous way to get something done or explain your troubles in a professional manner, not only are you not going to create a resentment, you're more likely to get what you want." So he evidently conveyed that to them in a civil manner. He is no longer working in that department. They moved him. So he's much happier there because he's learning something new. So he had a positive outcome. There's a right and there's a wrong, and just like laws in the community there's law in the corporate world. You've got to get that basic principle down, or you'll fail in any career you go into.

The mentor's concluding comments indicate some overlap between learning about a work organization and learning its norms. In this case, however, the mentor emphasized the youth's need to understand roles and power relationships and to communicate effectively.

Teamwork. Being able to work with others is essential in a contemporary work organization. Sixty-four percent of the control mentors used universal teaching behaviors to give basic information about teamwork; only one mentor used challenging behaviors. The following mentor narrated how he tried to get his protégé to reflect on the consequences of his attendance for the whole team. Note that this incident is also partly about rules and norms, but the mentor casts it in terms of teamwork.

A lot of our youth don't even realize the value of a team player and being a part of a team. They come as sophomores. If I was having a football team, they would realize that we're putting a team together to go play football. But they don't understand that we have projects that can't be completed in one day or two days. We have projects that take months, and they're just as valuable a team player on that project as the regular full-time worker. They have a responsibility to that team to show up for work and to get their work accomplished and not just try to get out of work, but when you get here, go to work, perform your work at the 100 percent quality that you're supposed to and get it done, because everyone else on that team is expecting you to do that. Because if you don't, then somebody's gonna have to come back and either take it apart because you didn't perform correctly or if you don't show up one day, somebody's gonna have to fill in for you to get that job done because they're depending on you to be there to be a team player. That's the way our projects work. Spring break is a week off from school. That's great, but that doesn't mean that's a week off from work. So it's real important to communicate to the team that you're not going to be here for spring break. It caused a problem because one student wasn't there to do the job that was expected of him. When he got back, I talked with him and made sure he understood that was not going to be acceptable behavior and put a write-up in his folder. He thought, *Hey, it's a week off school. If I don't go to school, I don't have to go to work.* At our next team meeting, we're going to ensure that everyone understands it. We try to go over this kind of information so that everyone is aware of it: the importance of being there, being dependable, being on time, and doing the quality of work so that people can depend on you and realize that you're part of the team and get that warm fuzzy as people rely on you.

Communication. About half of the control mentors (55 percent) used universal teaching behaviors to teach youth how to use appropriate technical, medical, or business vocabulary; to write clearly and accurately; to listen actively to understand information or directions; and to ask questions to learn, clarify, and solve problems. Only 7 percent used challenging behaviors. The following scenario illustrates how one mentor challenged a youth to use standard English daily in the workplace.

She's from an immigrant family, so English is not spoken in her home. She is from a poor community where there is more nonstandard English spoken. She described her goal as wanting to have good communication skills. What I had to have her understand was what constitutes communication: good communication, bad communication, standard communication, nonstandard communication. Why does one communicate at all? The reason why you are communicating influences how you communicate. So basically I told her that in an educational institution [that is, this workplace] you must model standards of good education, and so nonstandard English speaking is not allowed. When you come to work you're going to practice the Queen's English. And every time she would say "like" I would say, "We can't do that. You're going to break that habit." We would laugh about it. I live in the same neighborhood she lives in, and my whole family speaks nonstandard English. When I'm with them, I speak nonstandard English. That's how I have to communicate. If I go to a board meeting, the audience doesn't use that language. So my expectation was that she would use extremely proper standard English the whole time she was around. And I bugged her for two years, but she was good, really good. One thing I said to her was, "You're bilingual. You really speak two languages, and you're going to get real crafty identifying what's your intended audience and which you switch to, but you're going to be competent in both of them."

Nonwork

We found that 57 percent of the control mentors advised youth about issues not related to the workplace using universal behaviors; only 5 percent used challenging behaviors. Workplace mentors make personal choices about whether to advise youth about issues such as financial matters, ethical questions, and personal relationships. The engineer quoted earlier explained how his mentoring about rules and norms in the workplace developed a trust that extended the boundaries of the relationship beyond work. The relationship with his protégé evolved from teaching work tasks to conveying workplace rules and norms, then advising about a career path and even his social life. In the process, he does not just tell his protégé what to do but challenges him to think about what he is doing and the consequences of his choices.

As our relationship evolved and the work relationship evolved, I noticed that he was able to share more and more with me some other things that were going on in his life too. So I know that I did not really turn him off [by being firm]. I think it strengthened our relationship because the bottom line is that I think he felt that I had his best interests in mind. I was trying to prepare him for what he had to deal with in the future. When Jerome ran into problems, let's say in school or on the weekends, our relationship developed to such a point that he was sharing those things with me too. And I would ask him, "Why'd you do this, and why'd you do that?" I think after we got through talking, there were a lot of cases where he would say to me, "Yeah, I know. Didn't make much sense, did it?" So he was able to determine that. I didn't tell him.

This is a case of reflective questioning as a teaching behavior because the mentor asked the youth rather than telling him.

Recommendations

Our principal argument is that workplaces are especially appropriate and powerful settings for mentoring youth of high school age. To substantiate this point, we have described what good mentors do in high quality work-based learning settings. We now turn to the critical question of whether such workplace mentoring is feasible on a large scale. Is it possible to increase substantially the number of youth who benefit from a relationship with a workplace mentor? How would that be accomplished? How can high quality be maintained on a large scale? What policies and infrastructure can enable youth to strive to learn how to do good work, to participate in social organizations, and to act responsibly?

Freedman made a point that must be acknowledged first: mentoring is not free.[18] He warned against "fervor without infrastructure." When youth and adults meet each other in the normal course of their lives and then evolve a mentoring relationship by mutual consent, they make the necessary adjustments to their schedules, find transportation, and work out regular ways of communicating. If most youth naturally fell into mentoring relationships, as they may have in some golden age in the past, then programs would be unnecessary. But mentoring programs are needed precisely because young people and adults usually do not naturally come into contact under conditions that encourage and support mentoring relationships. Programs attempt to reconnect the generations that have been sundered by industrial and postindustrial conditions that separate learning, working, and family life. Investment is required to overcome the barriers these conditions pose.

Place mentoring within youth development initiatives

Mentoring is ideally part of a much larger initiative to foster youth development, and such initiatives ideally aim to build systems, rather than just programs. The School-to-Work Opportunities Act in fact called for the creation of systems, but this has proved a formidable goal. By definition, systems are inclusive, not merely special arrangements for a small group of youth.[19] One criterion for the inclusion of communities in our study was that they have high quality work-based learning programs large enough to give us access to fifteen new mentors. As it turned out, none of the eight communities we chose could ultimately identify fifteen new mentors, forcing us to include both new and experienced mentors in the study and demonstrating how rare large-scale work-based learning systems are. Work-based learning remains in most communities an opportunity open only to a small number of youth. Although the employer surveys conducted by Bailey, Hughes, and Barr found employers who said they were willing to provide work-based learning opportunities but had not been asked to do so,[20] our experience directing a youth apprenticeship demonstration project and the experiences of many other program operators have been just the opposite: that lack of employer commitment is the single most serious limiting factor in the number of youth who can be placed.

Overcoming that hurdle will lead to a range of opportunities—and challenges—some of which we will describe in this chapter. In an effective school-to-work system, mentoring and work-based learning are part of a set of opportunities that reinforce each other and cohere as a whole. For example, before choosing an internship in a particular career area, young people should have had field trips and job shadows in a range of workplaces, as well as good career information and advising, not to make a final choice about their life's work but to know why they are in a particular setting and what they hope to gain from it. In addition, their school courses, at least some of them, should support their learning at work by teaching some of the knowledge and skills required there and take advantage of it too, for example, by making assignments that draw on information and situations from the workplace.

When workplace mentoring is viewed as part of a comprehensive youth development system, it is easier to contemplate the notion of distributed mentoring. That is, rather than striving to match each youth with a single adult, educators and community leaders can think of mentoring as a role that can be performed by several different adults, not just one per youth. Bronfenbrenner's definition of a mentor clearly refers to an enduring pair.[15] However, if the goal of workplace mentoring is to teach technical, personal, and social competence, then it makes sense to share the task, at least to some extent. Representing the approach of many of the mentors we interviewed, one auto repair technician explained that he regularly placed his intern with other technicians who had different specialties, heating and air conditioning, for example, or electrical systems. In this way, the intern learned a broader range of skills than his mentor had to offer. This happens systematically when youth rotate through different departments and work assignments, as we recommend.[21]

Similarly, an intern or apprentice might turn to one mentor for advice on how to ask a supervisor for a change in assignment and another for information about the educational requirements for a physical therapist. This may be especially important when issues extend beyond the workplace. Some mentors strictly limit what they talk about to the workplace. Others, both because of their interns' needs and because of their interests and commitments, are open to a much wider ranging relationship. One mentor told us that she attended parent-teacher conferences with her apprentice because the apprentice's mother could not be counted on.

Build employers' commitment to mentoring

The near universality of work experience among high school students offers the tantalizing prospect that this common occurrence might foster youth development, that is, assure that youth gain more than monetary rewards for hourly work. If workplace mentors are to be made available to large numbers of youth in the United States, they will have to be found in a wider range of settings than such work-based learning programs as internships, apprenticeships, and cooperative education. Existing youth jobs are the most prevalent potential setting. If a substantial proportion of the jobs youth already have could be augmented as work-based learning opportunities, especially by encouraging adults in those workplaces to see themselves as mentors, the challenge of mentoring on a large scale could be met.

The presence of outstanding mentors in typical sites for youth jobs, including fast-food restaurants and retail stores, demonstrates that this is possible. Moreover, the goal need not be to convert all youth jobs. Some youth want and need only a chance to earn money. They have other opportunities to learn and to form mentoring relationships. Others can learn what they most need to know without any changes to the workplace, for example, punctuality, diligence, and customer relations.

Enrichment of youth jobs is especially promising for youth from low-income families who need work to supplement family income and may have few other opportunities. The major challenge to such enrichment is that employers hire youth for economic reasons, not to foster their development. Young people command low wages and are available evenings and weekends. Furthermore, large-scale employers of youth, notably fast-food restaurants, are organized specifically to be staffed by minimally trained people. Their procedures are so routinized and automated that literally a few minutes of training suffice to get a new worker started. This is what allows them to operate efficiently with inexperienced part-time staff and turnover that may exceed 100 percent per year. In such workplaces, asking for commitment to mentoring and work-based learning is asking for a total transformation of the standard way of treating employees. Such employers will attempt a transformation of this nature only if they believe their current mode is no longer profitable or if they anticipate a high rate of return on a new investment in young workers. Prospects are also influenced by the national and local labor markets, corporate culture, and managers' involvement in communitywide youth development initiatives. Walker has identified mentoring and after-school programs as initiatives for young adolescents that currently enjoy wide public support.[22] The strategies he recommends apply equally well to building a system of workplace mentoring for youth.

Workplace mentors are especially critical for disadvantaged youth. When young people grow up in stable families, with one or both parents regularly employed, and in neighborhoods where all the adults are working or could be if they chose, they are also more likely to have access to mentors through churches and other community organizations and through their families' social networks. Giving preference to disadvantaged youth in work-based mentoring programs is not simple, however. One complexity is that it identifies such programs and the youth in them with risk or worse, which may be stigmatizing and create a self-fulfilling prophecy. Second, identifying those in need is neither precise nor easy. Subjecting young people to a complex and intrusive selection process may not be the best way to recruit them. Finally, although youth from economically well-off families are less likely to need mentors, the association is merely probabilistic. The unspeakable carnage inflicted in recent years by a few boys from apparently good families on their teachers and classmates is only the most tragic illustration that the need for mentoring and other opportunities is not constrained by family income and parents' education.

These complexities are daunting, but so are the limits on access to mentors. Thus, a major challenge is to increase the number of mentoring opportunities available for those who need them most. Perhaps the best starting point is to resolve not to create programs that merely give those who are already thriving one more opportunity, while also working hard to avoid presumptions and stereotypes in matching youths in need with appropriate mentors.

To this end, it should be noted that paid youth jobs—as well as internships and apprenticeships—are not the only workplace settings in which young people can find mentors. Two other types of work-based learning that should be expanded and used in this way are service learning and youth-run businesses. Service learning is usually conceived as a way of teaching civic virtue along with other important lessons. It is, by definition, almost never paid. However, good service learning opportunities can build young people's connections with caring adults. Usually those are adult facilitators, but sometimes youth engaged in service learning in places like hospitals and nursing homes will form enduring relationships with those they are serving.

Youth-run businesses are especially important in places where jobs for youth are scarce, notably rural areas and inner cities. Among their advantages, they not only give young people a chance to learn about work but also to experience being managers. In their own businesses, young people assume a level of responsibility they would never be given in conventional workplaces. As a result, young people who may not know any adults who are even employed may come to think of themselves as having bright career prospects as managers, not just workers.

Actively recruiting mentors is important even when, as we have found to be the case, many adults are eager to play the role. In their masterly examination of "civic voluntarism," Verba, Schlozman, and Brady[23] tested a model of voluntarism with two main factors, motivation and capacity. However, they added a third, networks of recruitment, because they found that those with both the motivation and capacity to volunteer are more likely to do so if they are asked. It is important, therefore, to ask potential mentors to serve. It is even more important to select those most likely to be effective. Staff in a 1970s British program, Transition to Working Life, that matched a mentor called a "working coach" with a small group of youth developed a set of questions they would ask of business owners or managers.[24] In addition to asking about technical knowledge and skill, they asked, "Whom do your employees turn to for help when problems arise or a new technology is introduced?" In our demonstration project, we found it was essential to identify as mentors (or coaches) people high enough in the hierarchy to understand the workplace as a system. Workers who know only one job can teach only that job, which is not what we mean by mentoring.

Employers bear some of the program costs when mentoring occurs at work. Participating employers must be willing to authorize some of their best workers to devote substantial working time to their protégés. This may involve the mentor in a whole new range of commitments: attending training and support sessions, communicating with parents and teachers, reporting periodically on the protégé's progress, sharing ideas and experiences with other mentors. Before they agree to such redirection of workers' time, employers have to see their workplaces as learning organizations, not just for their current employees but for youth, only some of whom may become employees in the future. Interviews with mentors of youth apprentices in our demonstration project suggested that participating employers can expect to recoup this investment in at least two ways (in addition to training future workers and whatever benefits accrue in doing something good for their community). One is that youth quickly become skilled enough to provide substantial assistance to their mentors. Because they are paid at a low scale, appropriate to their status as worker-learners, their productivity can make up for the work their mentors would be doing without them. A second is that being a mentor serves as a form of professional development for some adults. Some mentors told us that by working with high school apprentices they developed skills they could use with adults under their supervision.

Train and support mentors

Orientation and training of mentors is an emerging art. By *orientation*, we mean conveying to mentors basic information about the program, its purposes and procedures, expectations, and communication channels. These are program specific. *Training*, on the other hand, is more general. Programs we have seen that are designed to train workplace mentors of youth frequently include information about adolescent development, training in giving feedback, and practice in communicating clearly. Little attention is devoted to teaching. We devised a training program that focused primarily on how to teach technical, personal, and social competencies, one that strongly emphasized the use of reflective questioning and problem solving as teaching methods. We identified mentors in eight sites and randomly chose four sites to offer training. Analysis of results to test the impact of the training is still under way. The low percentages of control mentors (without training) in our study who engaged in challenging teaching behaviors and the low percentages who said they taught youth at all about self-confidence, teamwork, communications, or systems indicate some of the needs that training can meet.

One training activity dealt directly with the issues we discussed earlier under the heading *nonwork*. We asked mentors to decide how far they are willing to go beyond the workplace in relation to some different issues that can arise and then to reflect with other mentors on the reasons for their choices. One point of the activity is that mentors should not feel compelled to become more involved with a youth than they wish to be. Another is that mentors can be good within the boundaries they set; they need not become surrogate parents to be effective. We introduced Bronfenbrenner's definition of a mentor in this context, as an ideal, but assured participants that they have valuable contributions to make even if they do not attain it.

Continuing support is another aspect of infrastructure in support of mentoring. Problems of all kinds arise that may jeopardize the program and relationship if they are not handled quickly and well. Some youth may need encouragement to articulate their concerns. Others need advice on how to act constructively, as in the case of the apprentice who planned to give his manager an ultimatum. Not all mentors have ready responses to such situations. Sometimes, problems in young people's personal lives or conflicts in their time commitments interfere with their reliability at work. A third party is often helpful in such situations. Many firms have employee assistance programs that connect youth to counselors. In our demonstration project, we adopted a case management approach to serious problems, bringing to the table not only the youth and mentor but parents, school representatives, and others as appropriate.

Transition to Working Life, the program that we mentioned earlier, employed human service professionals as advisers to workplace mentors, a practice borrowed by the Cornell mentoring demonstration project, Linking Up. Through group and individual meetings and phone calls, the advisers remained in touch with mentors, gave them confidence in their ability to perform the role, helped solve problems, and stimulated sharing among mentors, which may be the most important form of support.

The notion of distributed mentoring suggests another kind of training that we have not attempted: training youth to recruit mentors and to sustain relationships with them. One of the most important scientific sources supporting the value of mentoring is Werner and Smith's study of resilient children.[25] They found that the enduring presence of a caring adult, whether a parent, other relative, or someone else, was a constant in the lives of children who grew up severely deprived but nonetheless managed to achieve productive, secure lives for themselves as adults. Although their research design does not allow confirmation, they speculate that some children are better at attracting such adults. Young people might be taught, first, potential benefits of an adult mentor; second, what to look for in a prospective mentor; and third, how to negotiate the development of a mentoring relationship.

Notes

1. Mead, M. ([1928] 2001). *Coming of age in Samoa.* Reprint, New York: Harperperennial Library. pp. 164, 165, 170, 187.

2. Murnane, R. J., & Levy, F. (1996). *Teaching the new basic skills.* New York: Free Press. p. 32.

3. Bransford, J. D., et al. (Eds.). (2000). *How people learn: Brain, mind, experience, and school.* Washington, DC: National Academy Press. pp. 45–48. "Adaptive learning" is acquiring what these authors called "adaptive expertise."

4. Secretary's Commission on Achieving Necessary Skills. (1992). *Learning a living: A blueprint for high performance. A SCANS report for America 2000.* Washington, DC: U.S. Government Printing Office.

5. The term *preindustrial* includes societies organized around agriculture and those in which hunting and gathering provide sustenance. Unfortunately, it implicitly defines societies in relation to a dominant Western standard, as if all other societies are inevitably moving in one direction. Legitimate arguments can also be made against defining societies as industrial or information age. If we had more neutral but equally descriptive terms, we would use them.

6. Jordan, B. (1989). Cosmopolitan obstetrics: Some insights from the training of traditional midwives. *Social Science and Medicine, 28*(9), 925–944.

7. Schlegel, A., & Barry, H., III. (1991). *Adolescence: An anthropological inquiry.* New York: Free Press. p. 171.

8. Lave, J., & Wenger, E. (1991). *Situated learning: Legitimate peripheral participation.* Cambridge: Cambridge University Press.

9. Tierney, P., Grossman, J. B., & Resch, N. L. (1995). *Making a difference: An impact study of Big Brothers/Big Sisters.* Philadelphia: Public/Private Ventures.

10. Hamilton, S. F., & Hamilton, M. A. (1992). Mentoring programs: Promise and paradox. *Phi Delta Kappan, 73,* 546–550.

11. National Research Council. (1998). *Protecting youth at work: Health, safety, and development of working children and adolescents in the United States.* Washington, DC: National Academy Press.

12. Greenberger, E., & Steinberg, L. (1986). *When teenagers work: The psychological and social costs of adolescent employment.* New York: Basic Books.

13. Newman, K. S. (1999). *No shame in my game: The working poor in the inner city.* New York: Knopf and The Russell Sage Foundation.

14. Lund, L. (1992). *Corporate mentoring in U.S. schools: The outstretched hand* (Report No. 1007). New York: Conference Board.

15. Bronfenbrenner, U. Personal communication.

16. A grant from the National School-to-Work Office, a joint entity of the U.S. Departments of Education and Labor, supported this project. The findings reported here are the investigators'; readers should infer no endorsement by the sponsors.

17. Stasz, C., & Kaganoff, T. (1997). *Learning how to learn at work: Lessons from three high school programs.* Santa Monica, CA: RAND. p. 46.

18. Freedman, M. (1993). *The kindness of strangers: Reflections on the mentoring movement.* San Francisco: Jossey-Bass.

19. Hamilton, S. F., & Hamilton, M. A. (1999). *Building strong school-to-work systems: Illustrations of key components.* Washington, DC: National School-to-Work Office.

20. Bailey, T. R., Hughes, K. L., & Barr, T. (2000). Achieving scale and quality in school-to-work internships: Findings from two employers' surveys. *Educational Evaluation and Policy Analysis, 22,* 41–64.

21. Hamilton, M. A., & Hamilton, S. F. (1997). *Learning well at work: Choices for quality.* Washington, DC: National School-to-Work Office.

22. Walker, G. (2001). *The policy climate for early adolescent initiatives.* Philadelphia: Public/Private Ventures.

23. Verba, S., Schlozman, K. L., & Brady, H. E. (1995). *Voice and equality: Civic voluntarism in American politics.* Cambridge, MA: Harvard University Press.

24. Grubb Institute of Behavioural Studies. (1982). *Supporting young people in Transition to Working Life (TWL): TWL network in practice, 1978–1981* (Special Programmes Occasional Papers, No. 2). Moorfoot, Sheffield, England: Manpower Services Commission.

25. Werner, E. E., & Smith, R. S. (1992). *Overcoming the odds: High risk children from birth to adulthood.* Ithaca, NY: Cornell University Press.

MARY AGNES HAMILTON *is a senior research associate and codirector of the Youth and Work Program at Cornell University in Ithaca, New York.*

STEPHEN F. HAMILTON *is professor of human development and codirector of the Family Life Development Center at Cornell University in Ithaca, New York.*

Teachers are a centrally important yet often over-looked resource in the lives of youth. Teacher-student relationships, when properly harnessed, may emulate mentoring at its best. This chapter explores the teacher-student relationship and examines ways in which it can be enhanced to the benefit of youth and adults.

4

How schools can do better: Fostering stronger connections between teachers and students

Robert C. Pianta, Megan W. Stuhlman, Bridget K. Hamre

THERE IS LITTLE DOUBT that relationships between children and adults (parental and nonparental) play a prominent role in the development of competencies from the elementary school through the high school years.[1] Early on, such relationships form the developmental infrastructure on which other school experiences build, supporting adaptation of the child within the school and home

Note: The work reported here was performed under the Educational Research and Development Centers Program, PR/Award Number R307A60004, as administered by the Office of Educational Research and Improvement, U.S. Department of Education. However, the contents do not necessarily represent the positions or policies of the National Institute on Early Childhood Development and Education, the Office of Educational Research and Improvement, or the U.S. Department of Education, and readers should not assume endorsement by the federal government.

NEW DIRECTIONS FOR YOUTH DEVELOPMENT, NO. 93, SPRING 2002 © WILEY PERIODICALS, INC.

settings.[2,3] In adolescence, adult-child relationships function as structural supports and guides, sources of information and role modeling, emotional and social supports, and problem-solving resources.

Given that relationships with supportive nonparental adult mentors are both beneficial and in short supply, it seems logical that program developers and policymakers would strive to identify groups of adults who could develop such supportive relationships with youth. One underused and underdeveloped source of such adults is teachers and other adults in school settings.[4] Because young people spend a considerable amount of their time in school settings, facilitating the development of supportive adult-student relationships within the schools is a cost-effective option that requires minimal artificial manipulation on the part of interventionists. Not surprisingly, because they are public institutions in which nearly the entire population participates, schools are frequently a focus of efforts to promote health and reduce risk.[5] For example, Durlak and Wells found that 72.9 percent of all preventive intervention studies for children took place in schools, and 20 percent of change agents were teachers.[6] Yet for the most part, school reform efforts have focused less on infusing competence enhancement and preventive mental health strategies and more on putting in place accountability mechanisms. As a result, such preventive strategies remain a somewhat piecemeal phenomenon that appears more grafted onto existing structures than integrated into operational blueprints.

The similarities between teacher-student and mentor-youth relationships suggest that examining the nature and effects of student-teacher relationships, and the strategies used to build supportive student-teacher relationships, will hold promise for those who want to understand and exploit the value of mentoring relationships. Furthermore, such discussion logically integrates with arguments for development of competence enhancement and wellness strategies in natural settings in which children already operate, rather than relying on programs that target specific groups of children for services.[7] In the following sections, we will offer a conceptual model of student-teacher relationships and describe some promising strategies for enhancing the formation of close teacher-student relationships.

Factors affecting youth relationships with mentors and teachers

For the past ten years, my colleagues and I have focused on the student-teacher relationship system. Advancing a focus on that system as a key unit of analysis has provided an integrative conceptual tool for understanding development in school settings, much as a focus on parent-child relationships advanced the understanding of development in family settings.[4,8]

Ultimately, this focus on the student-teacher relationship system has helped inform efforts to construct school environments that better provide relationship resources to children.[4,9] To advance widespread benefits of mentoring, it could be quite helpful to examine theory on student-teacher relationships and identify similarities.

We view the primary components of the relationship system between teachers and students as involving four factors: (1) selected features of the two individuals themselves, (2) each individual's understanding of the relationship, (3) the processes by which student and teacher exchange information, and (4) the external influences of the systems in which the relationship is embedded.[10] Each of those factors is applicable to mentoring relationships as well.

First, relationships embody features of the individuals involved. These include biologically predisposed characteristics (such as temperament), personality, self-perceptions and beliefs, developmental history, and attributes such as gender or age. Findings from empirical studies of student-teacher relationships suggest that child and teacher gender and ethnic similarities can be related to the quality of the relationship;[11] gender and ethnic match are associated with less conflict and higher levels of closeness in these relationships. Such findings could be used to support policies that enhance the likelihood of such matching, but they also suggest a need for further research to understand the social and psychological mechanisms responsible for the match effect.

Relationships also involve each participant's views of the relationship and perceptions of the other's role in the relationship—what Bowlby and Sroufe and Fleeson call the members' representation of the relationship.[12,13] Consistent with evidence from the literature on parent-child relationships,[13,14] teachers' representations of relationships (particularly how they process negative emotion and experiences with the child) are related to how that teacher actually behaves with the child.[15] This consistent finding that teachers' representations of negativity in relation to a student have consequences for student and teacher outcomes is of considerable significance for policy and training. It is apparent that relationship negativity is a frequent experience for teachers (this may be different for mentors) and that such negativity erodes the value of the student-teacher relationship as a developmental resource. Of considerable concern in this regard is the fact that teachers have few, if any, opportunities to express and understand their negative experiences and to be trained in skills that can alter these representations and the interactions associated with them.

Relationships also include processes that serve to exchange information between the two individuals and serve a feedback function in the relationship system.[16] These processes include behavioral interactions, language, and communication, and they are critical to the smooth functioning of the relationship. For example, a teacher's sensitive behavior toward a child—responsiveness to the student's cues for help—can reduce the occurrence of problem behavior in the classroom among children likely to demonstrate such behavior.[17] To understand and improve such behavioral interactions, teachers and educators have to come to understand interactions with students from an organizational or systems point of view.[13,18]

Finally, relationships are themselves influenced by external factors such as class size, school climate, or grade-level transitions. For example, teachers are observed to provide a somewhat more positive emotional climate in the classroom and have more frequent interactions with specific students when class size is lower,[19] and students view their relationships with teachers more positively when students perceive the school climate as caring.[20] Similarly, elementary school children who report an emotionally close and warm relationship with their teacher view the school environment and climate more positively.[21] Researchers have found that, consistent with the view that middle school students need support from adult figures, teacher support is related to sixth-grade children's interest in school and to their pursuit of social goals.[22] These self-beliefs and motivations in sixth grade in turn predicted students' pursuit of social goals and grades in seventh grade. Importantly, the support that youth receive from their parents, peers, and teachers seemed to have additive—and thus fairly independent—effects. Support from teachers was uniquely associated with classroom functioning. Wentzel suggests the possibility that support in teacher-child relationships may be particularly salient at transition points, such as the transition from elementary to middle school.[22]

These relationship components (individual characteristics, representational models, information exchange processes) are themselves in dynamic reciprocal interactions. Behaviors of teacher and child toward one another influence their representations of the relationship,[15] and attributes of the child or teacher are related to teachers' perceptions of the relationship and the way teacher and child interact.[10,11] These relationship systems are also embedded in many other systems (such as classrooms, schools, and communities) and interact with systems at similar levels, such as families and peer groups. Thus, efforts to understand and improve relationships between students and teachers must attend to various component processes as well as ways in which these processes interact with one another and with external conditions.

It is difficult to disentangle the extent to which teacher-child relationships and school climate influence one another and the extent to which the balance of influence shifts as children grow older and their experiences are more widely distributed within a school. Nonetheless, there is ample evidence that school climate influences the quality of child-teacher relationships and vice versa.[23]

The way the school values and supports the emotional and social component of teacher-child interactions involves its view of the role and importance of child-teacher relationships.[20]

It is important to emphasize that adult-child relationships are asymmetric. There are differential levels of responsibility for interaction and quality that are a function of the discrepancy in roles and maturity of the adult and child, the balance of which changes and transforms across the school-age years.[24] Supportive relationships with teachers in high school are likely to be much less direct in their provision of help or resources to the child than they would be in middle or elementary school; instead, supportive teacher-student relationships in high school focus more on role modeling, problem solving, and enhancement of the youth's efforts at competent autonomy.[25]

In sum, we can integrate available evidence from diverse research by viewing the student-teacher relationship from a developmental systems perspective. Given the similarities between mentoring relationships and student-teacher relationships, it is quite likely that attention to similar factors could advance understanding of mentoring relationships. Unfortunately, in their comprehensive review of the literature on student-teacher relationships, Pianta, Hamre, and Stuhlman conclude that the available knowledge base on student-teacher relationships is lacking in certain key areas.[26] More research is needed that focuses on middle and high school students; on developmental studies of relationships across time, persons, and settings; and on systematic analysis of external factors as they relate to relationship quality and child outcomes.

Harnessing relational resources in school settings

In thinking about applying knowledge about student-teacher relationships across the many levels of organization and processes in schools, we approach the task with a bias toward the deployment of resources early and without eligibility requirements, with the distinct goal of enhancing wellness and strengthening developmental competencies for all children.[7] We believe there is ample evidence that, particularly for interventions involving schools, efforts reliant upon eligibility mechanisms fail to deliver resources early enough or to the wide range of children who might benefit from such resources. Indeed, it appears that professionals often focus on eligibility mechanisms themselves, draining financial, personnel, and intellectual resources away from the actual task of helping children.[7]

Clearly, interventions applied in the contexts in which a concern arises can be more effective agents of change than efforts at change that take place in a context remote from the problem at hand.[27] Thus, what we often think of as intervention might better be thought of in terms of designing educational environments to enhance the resources available for child development and produce change.[28] A dedicated focus on the relationship of the student and teacher clearly is a much different view than typical approaches to intervention that target improving the child's skills as a primary goal—and view the child as having the so-called problem.

From this perspective, the goal of intervention would be to enhance the fit between child and teacher in such a way that the child feels supported and the teacher feels effective, despite the child's problem behavior or lack of skills. Hamre and Pianta have demonstrated that the quality of student-teacher relationships uniquely forecasts students' academic and social outcomes independent of the teacher's view of the student's problem behavior or assessments of the child's cognitive ability.[29] In fact, we report that teacher-student negativity is more strongly predictive of child outcomes for children with problem behavior, thus demonstrating that the value of relationships may be even more important for vulnerable children.

One aspect of efforts to deploy resources to children that is addressed by focusing on natural settings is the length of exposure of the student to the resource being introduced.[6] It is the norm that resources are deployed to children in short-term bursts of six-week groups, semester-long mentoring, or placements that last a school year.[6] It is a laudable goal to accomplish significant developmental improvements in the short time frame of six weeks, particularly for children who have a long-standing history of concerns, yet most evaluations of these applications draw attention to the likelihood that effectiveness is diminished by short-term implementation. Strategically arranging relationships with adults in settings in which children "naturally," by virtue of their enrollment or participation in these settings, come in frequent contact with those resources over long periods of time may be preferable to shorter, albeit more intense, bursts of intervention through contact with less natural change agents such as therapists, outside professionals, and volunteers, no matter how well trained. The popularity and proliferation of schools' multiyear groupings of children with the same teacher may reflect this sense that children need exposure to developmental resources over a longer period of time than has been the typical assumption in intervention.

Within schools, efforts can be focused on the person or on the environment.[6] Felner, Favazza, Shim, and Brand argue that because developmental outcomes are based on transactions between individuals and environments, prevention and intervention should be aimed at both individuals and environments.[9] When promoting health for all children, alterations in the environment are preferable to alterations in individuals. That is yet another reason to view competence enhancement and risk reduction as distinct and to focus on the design of schools, classrooms, and teacher training.[7]

Improved relationships between teachers and students can be a focus of intervention efforts and a by-product of other efforts directed at children, teachers, classrooms, or schools. In particular, student-teacher relationships can be improved by targeting the organizational ethos and structure of the school or classroom as well as by targeting social interactions between teachers and children.

School and classroom approaches

Schools vary in terms of climate, ethos, values, and generalized expectations regarding the behavior of students and teachers. Furthermore, schools across the developmental span have very marked differences: middle schools are quite different from elementary schools, and both in turn vary considerably from high schools.[30] The climate of an environment influences children's confidence in their abilities,[31] teachers' beliefs about their efficacy,[32] and teaching practices that affect children's motivation and self-views.[33] Interventions at the level of school climate are complex and often diffuse. Some can involve restructuring of time and scheduling, allocation of space and teaching resources, and placement policies— as well as work related to school values, cultural issues, and staff support and involvement in decision making.[9] With a few exceptions, interventions at the school climate level are not directly focused on improving relationships between teachers and children. Nonetheless, these relationships can be profoundly affected because actions at this level often restructure student-teacher contact (in terms of frequency or stability) and quality (in terms of school climate).

In a comprehensive review of whole-school restructuring projects and their consequences for student mental health, Felner and colleagues concluded that often there is a "mismatch between the conditions and practices students encounter in grades K–12 and the developmental needs, readiness, and capacities of students."[9] Eccles and Roeser argue that as children move through elementary school and into middle school, the mismatch between their continuing needs for emotional support and the school's increasing departmentalization and impersonal climate grows.[24] Similarly, Harter discusses how relationships with teachers change from elementary to junior high school, becoming less personal, more formal, more evaluative, and more competitive.[30] These changes can lead to students having more negative self-evaluations and attitudes toward learning because the impersonal and evaluative nature of the relational context in middle school does not match well with the children's relational needs at that age—particularly for students who have low levels of intrinsic motivation. In this way, teacher-child relationships can actually exacerbate risk if they are either not positive or do not match with the developmental needs of the child.

One of these needs is to form functional, effective, supportive relationships with adults in the school setting.[24,34] A range of approaches with specific interventions that focus on the entire school shows promise for positively influencing child-teacher relationships.

Durlak and Wells' meta-analysis of primary prevention efforts supports the effectiveness of programs that modify the school environment and help children negotiate transitions.[6] One program, the Child Development Project (CDP), has been intensively involved with schools to promote social and moral development, a sense of community, and active caring for children within the school.[20,23] The need for schools to become caring communities is most commonly identified at the middle and high school levels, where preadolescent and adolescent disengagement and lack of connection to school values and social ethos are most marked.[20] However, CDP has been primarily involved with elementary schools. Although the actual implementation and end product of the CDP intervention mostly consists of a set of changes taking place at the classroom level, CDP involves extensive analysis and reshaping of the school environment as a prerequisite for changes sought at the classroom level.[20] In the view of CDP, interventions to address concerns such as caring, relationships, student autonomy, and values need to target both the classroom and school levels.

Prominent among the outcomes sought at the classroom level are opportunities for (1) pursuing common goals through student collaboration, (2) providing help and receiving help when needed, (3) reflecting and discussing one's own and other's perspectives and goals, and (4) practicing social competencies and exercising autonomy and making decisions. This approach involved changing discipline practices, teaching style (that is, emphasizing cooperative learning, making curriculum meaningful), and broadening the focus of schools so that goals include facilitating social and ethical dispositions, attitudes and motivations, and metacognitive skills. To promote these skills, Battistich and colleagues suggest that schools emphasize building and maintaining supportive, caring relationships between teachers and students, as well as among teachers and among students. More specifically, to build these relationships, Battistich and colleagues suggest activities such as having teachers and students share appropriate aspects of their personal lives, eat lunch together in small groups, and engage in other activities that communicate to students that teachers are genuinely interested and concerned about the range of the students' experiences and not only about their academic work. They also suggest that teacher-parent communication should be a priority so that teachers can have a greater awareness of what is going on in their students' lives. When schools prioritize these activities, teachers may know enough about their students to be able to adapt the curriculum so that it is relevant and interesting to them. Students will know that their teachers care for them and want to be in a collaborative partnership with them to help them attain their goals.

The approach used by the CDP at both the school and classroom levels has been evaluated in several studies. Battistich and colleagues summarize the evaluation of two years of implementation data in twenty-four highly diverse schools (twelve of them in a control group) through the middle school years.[20] The findings indicate positive changes in desired outcomes for the twelve CDP schools. CDP produced changes in teachers' observed warmth and supportiveness to students and low use of extrinsic control measures, both of which were in part responsible for children's increased engagement, influence in the classroom setting, and positive behavior toward peers and adults. Students reported an increase in their enjoyment of the classroom and motivation to learn, both of which are perceptions tied to the child's sense of relatedness within the classroom environment.[34]

Teacher-student interactions

In addition to projects studying school environments, some research focuses specifically on teacher-student interactions. Based on the success of fairly structured programs of parent consultation and training,[35] Pianta and Hamre and Pianta developed the Students, Teachers, and Relationship Support (STARS) system to help the teacher enhance the relationship with a specific student with whom the teacher reports a problem.[4,29] STARS is a multifaceted program that uses a supportive relationship with a consultant to target a teacher's representation of his or her relationship with a child and the teacher's behavior toward the student. Although primarily designed to address the needs of teachers of elementary and middle school students, STARS can also be a general relationship-building approach. As a result, components and principles of the STARS approach can be applied to youth and mentoring relationships.

The specific STARS technique directed at improving student-teacher interactions is banking time. In banking time, the teacher works with a consultant and implements a regular regimen of between five and fifteen minutes of individual time with a target student.[4,29] The name *banking time* is a metaphor for saving up positive experiences so that the relationship between teacher and student can withstand conflict, tension, and disagreement without deteriorating and returning to a negative state. Thus, the student and teacher can draw upon the accrued relationship capital and withdraw from the relationship resources that enable them to interact effectively in times of stress. The teacher's behavior in these sessions is highly constrained in order to produce changes in interaction and beliefs.

Banking time sessions emphasize the following four factors: (1) the regular occurrence of sessions, not contingent on the student's good behavior; (2) neutral verbalizations from the teacher that do not focus on the student's performance of skills; (3) relational messages from both teacher and student that help them define the relationship; (4) behavioral standards consistent with classroom standards. These principles of banking time sessions are very similar to teacher-child interaction therapy, in which teachers engage in nondirective sessions with children that are designed to enhance the quality of their relationship.[36] Many mentoring programs draw upon similar principles.

The STARS approach is designed to act on multiple components of the student-teacher relationship system, so it involves a set of other procedures that act on teachers' (and students') representations and beliefs. These include videotaping teachers' interactions with students in the classroom for review with the consultant, engaging in reflection on relationships through directed interviews, and analyzing classroom practices related to instruction and discipline. In combination with banking time sessions, these techniques are a comprehensive approach to intervention in student-teacher relationships, and they function more like a risk-reduction than a wellness approach.

Finally, Hughes and Cavell describe an intervention for aggressive children that includes enhancing the student-teacher relationship.[37] This intervention, called Primetime, espouses a relationship-based perspective on competence and attempts to reduce aggressive behavior by reorganizing the student's relational skills with parents, peers, and teachers. Primetime focuses on building a mentoring relationship with an adult who is a source of support and of skill training. Evaluations suggest that positive relationships between the children and the mentors were related to reduced levels of teacher-reported externalizing behavior (that is, acting out aggressive behavior).

Links between student-teacher relationships and mentoring

Relationships between children and teachers are marked by variation in both the extent of emotional and interactional involvement and the qualities of the emotional experience of that involvement. Negativity appears to be a particularly salient aspect of teachers' relationship experience, whereas emotional closeness, involvement, and support appear to be the most salient from the students' perspective. Using similar measurements and methods in the study of mentoring could help researchers understand whether these findings are unique to students and teachers or generalize to relationships with other nonparental adults.

Projects that focus on improving students' experience in school demonstrate that student-teacher relationships can be enhanced and that such enhancements are related to improvements in student competencies and perceptions as well as teacher confidence and beliefs. Sufficient information is available to design school environments that create a high likelihood that most, if not all, children can experience a positive relationship with a teacher (or other adult) and that schools can deliver more intensive and supportive relationship resources to more vulnerable children. Improving student-teacher relationships can be accomplished through both wellness and risk-reduction approaches. We cannot say how best to integrate mentoring into these models of environmental design and prevention strategies, but clearly mentoring can play an important role in ensuring the delivery of relational resources to children in schools.

Notes

1. Birch, S., & Ladd, G. (1996). Interpersonal relationships in the school environment and children's early school adjustment. In J. Juvonen & K. Wentzel (Eds.), *Social motivation: Understanding children's school adjustment* (pp. 199–225). Cambridge, MA: Cambridge University Press.

2. Howes, C. (2000). Social-emotional classroom climate in child care, child-teacher relationships, and children's second grade peer relations. *Social Development, 9,* 191–204.

3. Howes, C., Matheson, C. C., & Hamilton, C. E. (1994). Maternal, teacher, and child-care history correlates of children's relationships with peers. *Child Development, 65,* 264–273.

4. Pianta, R. C. (1999). *Enhancing relationships between children and teachers.* Washington, DC: American Psychological Association.

5. Cowen, E. (1994). The enhancement of psychological wellness: Challenges and opportunities. *American Journal of Community Psychology, 22*(2), 149–180.

6. Durlak, J., & Wells, A. (1997). Primary prevention mental health programs for children and adolescents: A meta-analytic review. *American Journal of Community Psychology, 25*(2), 115–152.

7. Cowen, E. (1999). In sickness and in health: Primary prevention's vows revisited. In D. Cicchetti & S. L. Toth (Eds.), *Rochester Symposium on Developmental Psychopathology,* vol. 9, *Developmental Approaches to Prevention and Intervention* (pp. 1–24). Rochester, NY: University of Rochester Press.

8. Bronfenbrenner, U., & Morris, P. A. (1998). The ecology of developmen-

tal processes. In W. Damon & R. M. Lerner (Eds.), *Handbook of child psychology: Theoretical models of human development* (5th ed., pp. 993–1028). New York: Wiley.

9. Felner, R., Favazza, A., Shim, M., & Brand, S. (in press). Whole school improvement and restructuring as prevention and promotion: Lessons from project STEP and the project on high performance learning communities. *Journal of School Psychology.*

10. Pianta, R., et al. (in press). Observed quality of the kindergarten classroom environment: Description and relations with teacher, family, and school characteristics and child outcomes. *Elementary School Journal.*

11. Saft, E. W., & Pianta, R. C. (in press). Teachers' perceptions of their relationships with students: Relations with child and teacher characteristics. *School Psychology Quarterly.*

12. Bowlby, J. (1969). *Attachment and loss.* Vol. 1, *Attachment.* New York: Basic Books.

13. Sroufe, L. A., & Fleeson, J. (1988). Attachment and the construction of relationships. In W. Hartup & Z. Rubin (Eds.), *Relationships and development.* Hillsdale, NJ: Erlbaum.

14. Main, M., Kaplan, N., & Cassidy, J. (1985). Security in infancy, childhood, and adulthood: A move to the level of the representation. In I. Bretherton & E. Waters (Eds.), *Growing points in attachment theory and research* (pp. 66–104). Monographs of the Society for Research in Child Development, vol. 50, nos. 1–2, serial no. 209. Cambridge, MA: Blackwell.

15. Stuhlman, M., & Pianta, R. (in press). A narrative approach to assessing teacher-child relationships: Associations with behavior in classrooms. *School Psychology Review.*

16. Lerner, R. M. (1998). Theories of human development: Contemporary perspectives. In W. Damon & R. M. Lerner (Eds.), *Handbook of child psychology: Theoretical models of human development* (5th ed., pp. 1–24). New York: Wiley.

17. Early, D., et al. (2000). *Maternal sensitivity and child wariness in the transition to kindergarten.* Manuscript submitted for publication.

18. Hinde, R. (1987). *Individuals, relationships, and culture.* Cambridge: Cambridge University Press.

19. NICHD Early Child Care Research Network. (2001, April). *Observations in first-grade classrooms: The other side of school readiness.* Paper presented at the biennial meeting of the Society for Research in Child Development, Minneapolis, MN.

20. Battistich, V., Solomon, D., Watson, M., & Schaps, E. (1997). Caring school communities. *Educational Psychologist, 32*(3), 137–151.

21. Murray, C., & Greenberg, M. T. (2000). Children's relationship with teachers and bonds with school: An investigation of patterns and correlates in middle childhood. *Psychology in the Schools, 38*(5), 425–446.

22. Wentzel, K. (1998). Social relationships and motivation in middle school: The role of parents, teachers, and peers. *Journal of Educational Psychology, 90*(2), 202–209.

23. Solomon, D., et al. (1996). Creating classrooms that students experience as communities. *American Journal of Community Psychology, 24*(6), 719–748.

24. Eccles, J., & Roeser, R. (1998). School and community influences on human development. In M. H. Bornstein & M. E. Lamb (Eds.), *Developmental psychology: An advanced textbook* (4th ed., pp. 503–554). Hillside, NJ: Erlbaum.

25. Axelman, M. J. (2000). The relational experiences of African-American adolescents and the role of significant adults: An examination of teenage lives during the transition to high school. Unpublished doctoral dissertation, University of Virginia. *Dissertation Abstracts International: Section B: Sciences and Engineering, 60*(11-B), 5809.

26. Pianta, R. C., Hamre B. K., & Stuhlman, M. W. (in press). Relationships between teachers and children. In W. M. Reynolds & G. E. Miller (Eds.), *Comprehensive Handbook of Psychology*, vol. 7, *Educational Psychology*. New York: Wiley.

27. Henggeler, S. W. (1994). A consensus: Conclusions of the APA task force report on innovative models of mental health services for children, adolescents, and their families. *Journal of Clinical Child Psychology, 23*, 3–6.

28. Adelman, H. S. (1996). Restructuring education support services and integrating community resources: Beyond the full service school model. *School Psychology Review, 25*, 431–445.

29. Hamre, B., & Pianta, R. (2001). Early teacher-child relationships and the trajectory of children's school outcomes through eighth grade. *Child Development, 72*(2), 625–638.

30. Harter, S. (1996). Teacher and classmate influences on scholastic motivation, self-esteem, and level of voice in adolescents. In J. Juvonen & K. Wentzel (Eds.), *Social motivation: Understanding children's school adjustment* (pp. 199–225). Cambridge: Cambridge University Press.

31. Cauce, A. M., Comer, J. P., & Schwartz, D. (1987). Long-term effects of a systems-oriented school prevention program. *American Journal of Orthopsychiatric Association, 57*, 127–131.

32. Bandura, A. (1994). *Self-efficacy: The exercise of control.* New York: Freeman.

33. MacIver, D. J., Reuman, D. A., & Main, S. R. (1995). Social structuring of school: Studying what is, illuminating what could be. In M. R. Rosenzweig and L. W. Porter (Eds.), *Annual review of psychology, 46*, 374–440.

34. Connell, J. P., & Wellborn, J. G. (1991). Competence, autonomy, and relatedness: A motivational analysis of self-system processes. In R. Gunnar & L. A. Sroufe (Eds.), *Minnesota symposia on child psychology* (vol. 23, pp. 43–77). Hillside, NJ: Erlbaum.

35. Barkley, R. (1987). *Defiant children: A clinician's manual for parent training.* New York: Guilford Press.

36. McIntosh, D. E., Rizza, M. G., & Bliss, L. (2000). Implementing empirically supported interventions: Teacher-child interaction therapy. *Psychology in the School, 37*(5), 453–462.

37. Hughes, J., & Cavell, T. (1999). School-based interventions for aggressive children: Primetime as a case in point. In S. Russ & T. Ollendick (Eds.), *Handbook of psychotherapies with children and families*. New York: Kluver Academic/Plenum Publishers.

ROBERT C. PIANTA *is a professor in the Curry School of Education's Programs in Clinical and School Psychology at the University of Virginia.*

MEGAN W. STUHLMAN *is a doctoral student in the Curry School of Education, University of Virginia.*

BRIDGET K. HAMRE *is a doctoral student in the Curry School of Education, University of Virginia.*

Schools have increasingly implemented advising programs as a means of linking students with caring adults. Although this approach is promising, its success depends on adequate funding; the full commitment of administration, staff, and parents; and a thoughtful definition of the procedures for achieving the goals.

5

Can advising lead to meaningful relationships?

Nancy Rappaport

MENTORING PROGRAMS are often enthusiastically endorsed by community organizations, corporations, and government entities as an effective way to nurture children. However, vulnerable children who frequently have positive mentoring experiences show only modest improvement in academic performance, self-esteem, and school attendance, and this illustrates the need for guarded optimism.[1] Even in the best of circumstances, when mentors are carefully trained and matched with children, these types of one-on-one relationships are challenging to sustain.[2] Simply put, relationships between children and mentors have limitations stemming from logistical difficulties, a dearth of qualified volunteers, the absence of a prior history, and so on. Often, they can seem contrived and therefore susceptible to premature termination.[3]

NEW DIRECTIONS FOR YOUTH DEVELOPMENT, NO. 93, SPRING 2002 © WILEY PERIODICALS, INC.

Obstacles to student-teacher bonding in traditional schools

Given that children spend the majority of the day in a school set-ting, researchers and program developers have sought to forge con-structive relationships in this environment as an alternative to mentoring.[4,5] Many elementary schools have successfully provided students and teachers with opportunities to build and maintain rela-tionships. A quality of caring and attentiveness pervades these schools, as does the recognition that relationships with adults are critical in children's development.[6]

Unfortunately, many schools, especially middle schools and high schools, are structured in ways that make it difficult for students to develop stable relationships with teachers.[7] Researchers have noted that middle school students tend to have few positive inter-actions with teachers outside of instruction and feel less secure with their teachers than do children in elementary school.[8] The growing emphasis on standardized testing in middle and high school often gives rise to rigid curricular demands that constrain teachers and leave little room for the kinds of activities that typi-cally draw them closer to their students. The structure of middle schools often prevents the formation of genuine, trusting rela-tionships between teachers and students.[9,10] Yet studies of social support demonstrate that perceived support from teachers is a sig-nificant predictor of young adolescents' motivation and academic successes.[5]

To address these obstacles, educators have tried to initiate some structural school reform efforts to create more responsive school communities. They have used school reform efforts that address school and classroom climate. They have also played host to school-based mentoring programs, which are coordinated inter-nally or sponsored through intermediaries like Big Brothers Big Sisters of America. Yet the orchestration of thousands of pairings of mentoring relationships for students presents substantial diffi-culties in any educational environment. The number of students in need of warm supportive adults far exceeds the availability of volunteers who are willing to give up a portion of their workday to meet on school grounds.

Strengths and weaknesses of school advising programs

A more practical approach might be to increase the capacity for caring, stable, informal interactions within school settings by fortifying existing ties. To this end, advising programs have proliferated in many schools as an institutional antidote to the lack of opportunities for students to form close relationships with teachers. Leading professional organizations have endorsed advising programs as a promising way to allow every student to be known by a caring adult.[11] About two-thirds of the schools in the United States that include grade seven have one homeroom or group advisory period, although no accurate national data exist concerning the precise prevalence of advising. In one survey of approximately two thousand school principals, advising programs were found most frequently in schools in the Northeast, in urban areas with higher percentages of minority students and school families below the poverty line.[12]

Calculating the frequency of advising programs is further complicated by the fact that the term *advising* has no universal definition.[13] Advisers at some schools meet weekly with students and cover administrative tasks, whereas other advisers meet daily and provide social and emotional support. The only common denominator is that the students are a captive audience and that the advising occurs during the school day, usually drawing on teachers to be the advisers. Although the content varies in terms of the emphasis on educational or social goals, ideally the adviser provides emotional grounding and acts as a role model. Usually, advisers are primarily responsible for a small group of ten to fifteen students.

In alternative public schools and private schools, well-planned advising programs have made a difference in students' engaged behavior and student performance, and financial and staff resources are allocated to sustain this type of support.[14] These schools are less restrained by the economics of providing the smaller teacher-student ratios that allow the teachers to take on this additional responsibility.[2] However, the larger advising movement in public schools has not been consistently executed, funded, or sufficiently evaluated to ensure similar success. Teachers and administrators in such schools sometimes resist efforts that they view to be too big a drain on resources or as destabilizing to the system.[9]

As with many other educational reforms,[10] advising was adopted in many schools with little attention to the infrastructure required or with any means of evaluation. Advising programs, for example, require a significant reallocation of resources, time, and staff professional development to expand teachers' roles.[15] Moreover, few programs evaluated their efforts. Indeed, a survey of nineteen hundred schools showed that 47 percent of schools initiated advising in fifth through ninth grade, yet what little outcome data were collected on their efforts is largely consigned to unpublished reports.[13,16] The published data are usually brief surveys and do not capture how the advising relationships influence students' behavior. Primarily, information available focuses on the logistical steps for implementing advising and examines how schools prioritize what gets covered in advising.[13] Although the information makes frequent references to the importance of the adviser's understanding of child development and group dynamics,[17,18] it gives no guidelines that effectively assess the differences between successful and failed advising efforts.

Enhancing the capacity of large public schools to promote teacher-student relationships through advising is a complicated process, and numerous challenges remain. This chapter draws on my experience, systematic process observation of groups, and ongoing focus groups with support staff in an urban high school that has tried to institutionalize caring and enhance student engagement by implementing an advising program. My observations as a child and adolescent psychiatrist highlight important questions about the nature of the mentoring relationship as well as the predictable obstacles and necessary commitment of all parties as crucial to sustain an advising program. These observations provide a gateway to the discussion of the types of obstacles that schools may confront, and may ultimately lead to qualitative descriptions of successful advising groups.

The study

For the past six years, an urban public high school in a Northeastern city adjacent to a university has made a concerted effort to provide an advising program for its students. The initiative is based on the premise that constructive relationships between students and adults can enhance learning. The belief has firm grounding in the research literature, which has consistently highlighted the protective benefits of support relationships.[19] The impetus for this effort stemmed from recognition of the vulnerabilities of the diverse body of students attending the high school. A districtwide analysis of school performance revealed that approximately one-third of the students fail at least one course every semester. The failure rate for minorities was even higher: 41 percent for African American students and 43 percent for Latino students. Of the more than two thousand students who attended the public high school, approximately 60 percent are racial or ethnic minorities; more than half are eligible to receive free lunches; and one-third speak a first language other than English.

The advising program is being phased in as part of ongoing restructuring, which includes heterogeneous student grouping, interdisciplinary teaming, and structured time for staff collaboration. The advising has expanded to all four years, and school personnel anticipate that the adviser will stay with the same students for the duration of their enrollment at the high school. The students see their advisers two days a week during a regular class period. The evaluation of the program has revealed promising preliminary findings, including high satisfaction ratings from teachers and students alike. We are currently tracking a broader range of indices (for example, grade point average, suspensions, and detentions) that are assumed to be linked to the redesign efforts. In the following sections, I will describe several of the issues that arose throughout the implementation process. My hope is that these observations will help to create a research agenda for this important educational reform.

Implementation challenges

Leadership

The success of the advising process appears to depend to a large extent on whether the program has a leader who champions the cause and tenaciously works through the obstacles and logistics. This leader can keep the process energized and strategize about how to overcome the structural impediments that inevitably arise when institutional inertia impedes the school innovation. As McDonald points out, in successful redesign efforts the committed leader must take actions in small incremental steps, exercise charisma, possess an almost evangelical faith balanced with skepticism, and encourage a certain defiance of the status quo.[20] The leader must also hold a position of power in order to maintain the vision while attending to the myriad of details that can derail the systemic advising effort.

Ideally, students should be assigned to advisers who will already see them during the course of the school day in academic courses, homerooms, or cocurricular activities.[21] Also ideally, schools would have the resources to choose staff members to participate in advising according to each school's values. But in reality, resources are limited, and public schools are under pressure to keep a tight schedule and justify that time is spent on learning, in accordance with state directives. Advising programs can succeed in such an environment only with active, consistent leadership.

Many of the ills of an advising effort saddled with poor leadership became evident over the years of this study. To begin, this high school has had four different principals in eight years, generally contributing to the rhetorical endorsement of advising without overseeing adequate and consistent implementation. Because of the flexible nature of advising, the time tended to become a dumping ground for ambitious agendas without proper attention to the resources and training required to provide competent execution. One year, the advising time was used partly for preparation for high-stakes standardized tests, with no guidance for advisers as to how to manage this. Another year, the scheduling was so difficult that as many as twenty-eight students were in each group, far more than the recognized ideal size of eight to twelve.[22] Advising, like mentoring, is hard work. If leadership is insufficient to provide the infrastructure to bring staff and students together, then the half-hearted advising effort that will no doubt arise can contribute to pervasive cynicism. This inconsistent effort presents the deceptively complacent facade that an innovation is being executed, even when it is fundamentally and fatally flawed.

The importance of leaders' active facilitation and attention to detail is illustrated in the following vignette, in which an advising effort actually reinforces the marginalization of disengaged students. I was observing a group of eighteen high school students as an adviser valiantly tried to maintain a coherent discussion about discipline and graduation requirements. During the session, I identified seven informal ringleaders who had bonded over derailing any positive interaction with the adviser, disrupting the class by ripping up paper and dropping their pencils. Dealing with one troublemaker is challenging enough; with seven, it is almost impossible. After the session, the adviser, a seasoned veteran teacher, expressed her disillusionment at the possibility of connecting to these students. I explored with her various possibilities, but emphasized that she must divide the group into two. Fortunately, she was committed enough to be willing to give up her prep period to make this possible. But for three weeks, despite persistent appeals and directives from the principal, the assistant principal did not generate the changed schedule for the students.

Finally, the groups were divided. The adviser subsequently discovered that she was then able to motivate these students, including one student who later came with the adviser to a school committee to give a testimonial. He told the committee that advising was his first positive experience in school. He grew up in a neighborhood where drug dealing was a major occupation. His adviser was the only adult who had encouraged him to invest in school and take academic risks; he was able to do this because she cared. This example reflects the tenuous nature of advising. A school needs to be flexible when relationships are in trouble and provide leadership to recognize the necessary modifications of structure.

Addressing school structure, culture, and climate

Advising is easier to implement if the school not only examines the rules and roles of advisers but also explores the school's unconscious and conscious resistance to setting aside time for this activity. To the extent that administrators convey reluctance, beliefs and values undermine positive relationships with students. Researchers usually recommend that schools allocate anywhere from six months to two years of preparation before starting advising, in order to assess teacher skill level, outline increased responsibilities, and develop the advising curriculum.[16] But despite this preparation, advising programs still often have difficult beginnings or are eventually dropped. Many people acknowledge that of all the innovations introduced in middle schools, adviser-advisee programs are the most difficult to implement and to maintain.[17]

In examining the difficulty of sustaining educational innovations, one must pay greater attention to the individual questions, needs, and opinions that arise among teachers in response to the innovations.[23] Many teachers have a level of discomfort about being advisers. Their reluctance may originate from multiple concerns: they are inadequately prepared, lack the necessary skills, or perhaps are unclear about what is expected from them. Other reasons for this lack of enthusiasm include inadequate staff development, reluctance to stray from teaching subject matter, or the fact that some teachers just do not want to be forced to share with their students.[22] Some staff are reluctant to invest emotionally in students. Some worry about balancing sympathy to students' barriers to learning with the necessity to uphold stringent academic standards. Also, some teachers see it as problematic and contrived to create artificial emphasis on emotional bonding, as it erodes formal boundaries and emphasis on the teachers' tasks of imparting knowledge and necessary skills. They may feel that the process of building strong connections to students should derive from sharing enthusiasm about the subject matter and class participation instead of isolating out the advising from the student performance.

Adopting advising in a school can also be threatening because it evokes latent anxieties about the school's difficulties. Powell examined an all-school effort to alter school culture, called Family Group, which structured groups facilitated by school adults.[18] She interpreted the school staff's reluctance to change as a fear of losing the social distance offered by a school's administrative roles to manage strong feelings, anxiety, and unspoken difficulties. This social defense promotes policies and responses that maintain the status quo, and it maintains structural barriers that interfere with building strong teacher-student bonds. In determining the readiness of a school to adopt advising, understanding the characteristics of the staff and designing the infrastructure to address their concerns are useful. Schools must provide a forum for meaningful discussions in which staff can explore their apprehensions. In fact, such forums can serve as a template for staff in the construction of their advising discussion with students. In weekly focus groups that I led for two years, many teachers shared feelings of being devalued, overwhelmed, and tired. They approached students with a level of resignation and futility because they lacked the needed support from the broader system. Many veteran teachers told me that whereas they once invested time and effort in building relationships with students, they now felt more consumed by responsibilities such as caring for their own young children or elderly parents.

Creating a protected time in which teachers could reflect on these feelings served ultimately to increase their investment and generosity with students.

At this high school, teachers and administrators had the opportunity to discuss and explore the problems they anticipated confronting with their students in advising. Some teachers worried that if students did not have definite guidelines, in an unstructured setting they would reveal overwhelmingly intimate details about their lives (for example, abuse, abortions). Some school committee members and parents angrily believed that this initiative was a surreptitious effort by school adults to supplant the role of the family.

Nevertheless, the program went forward, and what really happened was the opposite of what many feared. When teachers started advising groups of students, it was the teenagers who were cautious and did not share readily. The most common problem for advisers in fact was not an outpouring of deep secrets but rather dealing with the suspicious silence they encountered in 80 percent of groups in the initial phase.[15]

Unfortunately, this was an attitude that the advisers themselves sometimes fostered. One adviser decided to wait almost two months to see how long it would take for the advisees in her group even to introduce themselves to each other. She seemed almost to revel in the futility of students taking the initiative, let alone developing meaningful relationships. This seemingly puzzling response becomes clearer if we interpret it as acknowledging that schools may be unconsciously designed to keep students at a distance and that some teachers are happy to perpetuate this standoff.

Another aspect of understanding the readiness of schools to adopt an advising program is to analyze the school climate, particularly with respect to power dynamics and the process of decision making. Schools have a variety of operating principles that both reflect and contribute to the interpersonal climate within them. For example, Tremlow and colleagues evaluate the covert power dynamic present in schools that are experiencing violence.[24] This power dynamic may be subtle and unconsciously motivated, and it may pervade all levels, wherein students, teachers, and administrators "abusively coerce others repeatedly through humiliation and mockery; the stronger, more dominant personality coercing a weaker, more submissive personality." Staff members may consciously or unconsciously participate in escalating conflict, and schools often do not hold them responsible for their actions.[25] Thus, in fortifying the role between teachers and students, identifying cases of a covert power dynamic in which violent students are implicitly mirroring the aggressive climate that staff can sometimes perpetuate can be helpful.

A critical aspect of adolescents' development is how they see themselves as alternating between omnipotent, powerful, and powerless.[26] A useful step in advising is to explore how power is distributed in the school so that students can analyze their perceptions about power. This kind of discussion can facilitate students developing their sense of self-efficacy.[27] In my observations of advising groups, a recurrent theme was students' discussion about their perceived sense of injustice in the school or their conflict with certain teachers. Some teachers struggled with the notion that if they explored this with students, they were betraying their colleagues' confidence and endorsing students' belligerent attitudes. (One teacher went so far as to eavesdrop on another adviser and then express outrage that this adviser initiated a discussion about the students' worst experiences with teachers.)

In my observation of an advising group, I have found that open discussion can have positive results. One teacher was particularly adept at examining the students' interpretation of the power dynamics operating in the school. His approach was to listen to students' challenge of authority. He did not feel compelled to fix their struggle but encouraged students to take initiative. The teacher asked, "Who has had trouble with a teacher?" The students all became animated, and everyone raised his or her hand. Students began to yell out names, but the adviser was firm that he did not want to hear names of teachers. A quiet girl asked, "What do you do if a teacher is rude and seems to single you out?" The adviser corrected her by saying that the student feels that the teacher is rude. The student persisted and said that no, the teacher was rude.

Another student said, "Fire her. She is a bad teacher." The adviser wittily replied, "And I am sure that you are all angels," gently reminding them thus that there are two sides to every story. He then suggested that the key to resolving a conflict is finding the right timing and offered himself as an ally. He also suggested that students not be insulting and that they try to stick to concrete examples. So even though a group may not come to any resolution, ongoing advising meetings can offer opportunities for students to explore constructive ways of problem solving in the presence of an attentive adult.

Another of the great challenges facing advising innovation is that an evaluation of its successes is often held to an unfairly high standard. A key discussion centers on the feedback loop or how the school community decides who is competent or available to participate in advising. Ten years ago, the former superintendent put a halt to the entire program because she saw a few teachers at a local coffee shop at a time when they should have been conducting advising. During the more recent advising initiative that I observed, many teachers were concerned that an adviser was using the advising time for a glorified study hall. It seems curious that the administrators so quickly jumped to these incidents as an impetus to close down shop rather than an added incentive to monitor and support advisers. These aberrant advisers acted as a lightning rod for institutional ambivalence.

This ambivalence is paralleled by the anger, disappointment, and paralysis that students feel when they have incompetent advisers. As in mentoring, advising relationships lie along a vast continuum, and schools must not endorse or perpetuate a charade of commitment when, in fact, the adults' involvement is reluctant, disengaged, or unpredictable. Frequently, students at the high school complained that advising was a waste of time, that nothing was accomplished in the process. I found that usually it was the teachers who had difficulty with class management, organization, and ground rules in their ordinary classrooms who could not create an emotional home base in their advising groups. In one situation I observed, students recognized that their adviser was problematic because she had already been transferred from five schools. Although the students did not want to hurt the adviser's feelings and knew she did not take criticism well, they felt that she yelled too much. Sadly, they also recognized that they needed an adult to help them listen to each other and prepare them to do well academically. This case illustrates the fact that for advising to be successful, schools must install a reliable system for receiving and dealing with feedback from students.

Although some advisers may be uncomfortable with the sense of trying to win a popularity contest with their students, schools would be prudent to develop mechanisms for both observation and feedback. The absence of data to quantify predictably successful advising relationships has led to an overreliance on anecdotes from students and teachers alike. Evaluations of mentoring programs suggest that modest expectations are in order, as the proportion of matches that turn into significant relationships is at best between one-third to two-thirds overall.[2]

Supervision

Another challenge the advising relationship presents is providing assistance to the advisers themselves. Without adequate supervision, advisers might still provide students guidance but be unable to address and resolve difficult situations. I found many teachers aware of this weakness and receptive to suggestions about how to handle personality conflicts or challenging students. Often, advisers appreciated the opportunity for supervision when teacher-student relationships were particularly threatened. Sometimes, participating in role modeling in which a group of teachers could act out particularly difficult situations operated as the impetus for reflection. Other times, teachers would share their reaction to various predictable stages of the year, such as the end of the school year. They could then use their insight to respond more empathetically to the emotions their students were experiencing. In still another case, when an advising group was in crisis, drawing on the resources of a clinician to examine the problematic situation provided the necessary momentum to turn it around.

Advisers sometimes preferred not to discuss feelings of ambivalence or frustration with the process, perhaps in the hopes that these would eventually dissipate. An example was an adviser who was injured when he was trying to protect two students in a fight that broke out during an advising period. After returning to the group, the adviser chose not to address the fight with students because he was not sure what to say. The group had been functioning well, but increasingly students were excusing themselves early to go to lunch and avoiding any controversial topic. When I discussed with the adviser his concerns, he said that he was ambivalent. The expelled student had violated a school rule and injured the teacher, but he had been under tremendous pressure. His father was awaiting a transplant, and a snide remark by another student provoked him. The adviser did not want to excuse the assault, but he felt sympathetic to the student and did not want the situation to escalate. With my encouragement, he revisited with the group the ground rules for safety, explained the fighting incident, and shared his sadness. The group was then able to reestablish a level of cohesiveness and use the incident as a catalyst for a productive discussion about anger.

Final implications

When a school institutes advising to provide caring, how this time will be used is not always predictable. Once in a while, staff and students use it as a venue for profound discourse where meaningful exchanges occur. It is important not to treat these moments as happenstance but to realize that the opportunity arises out of the school's preparation and investment in shifting how the teachers and students see each other. In one group I observed, an adviser had inoperable cancer. Despite his illness, he was primarily concerned about providing for his advisees. The contract between the students and this teacher was that the students recognized that his caring for them as he was dying motivated them to invest in their future.

The effort of school communities to build strong relationships is a worthwhile endeavor, although the jury is still out on how many will ultimately succeed. As with mentoring programs, the success of advising programs is likely to hinge on the extent to which school personnel make a commitment to developing strong, sustained relationships and to putting in place the necessary resources to ensure adequate infrastructure, supervision, and thoughtful analysis. Within this context, baseline and follow-up data need to be collected to determine how advising programs are operating and to identify the range of effects they are having. Finally, it would be useful to have qualitative descriptions of successful advising groups. Journals and field notes by teachers and students can provide insights into how change occurs. Adequately supported, this type of school effort has the potential to address the needs of adolescents for meaningful connections with supportive adults.

Notes

1. Rhodes, J., Grossman, J., & Resch, N. (in press). Agents of change: Pathways through which mentoring relationships influence adolescents' academic adjustment. *Child Development*.

2. Freedman, M. (1993). *The kindness of strangers: Adult mentors, urban youth, and the new volunteerism.* San Francisco: Jossey-Bass.

3. Grossman, J. B., & Rhodes, J. E. (in press). The test of time: Predictors and effects of duration in youth mentoring programs. *American Journal of Community Psychology*.

4. Pianta, R. C. (1999). *Enhancing relationships between children and teachers.* Washington, DC: American Psychological Association.

5. Doll, B., & Lyon, M. (1998). Risk and resilience: Implications for the delivery of educational and mental health services in schools. *School Psychology Review, 27,* 348–363.

6. Comer, J. P., Haynes, N., Joyner, E., & Ben-Avie, M. (1996). *Rallying the whole village: The Comer process for reforming education.* New York: Teachers College Press.

7. Eccles, J., Midgley, C., Wigfield, A., Buchanan, C. M., Reuman, D., Flanagan, C., & MacIver, D. (1993). Development during adolescence: The impact of stage-environment fit on young adolescents' experiences in schools and in families. *American Psychologist, 48,* 90–101.

8. Cauce, A. M., Mason, C., Gonzales, N., Hiraga, Y., & Liu, G. (1994). Social support during adolescence: Methodological and theoretical considerations. In F. Nestmann & K. Hurrelmann (Eds.), *Social networks and social support in childhood and adolescence: Prevention and intervention in childhood and adolescence* (pp. 89–108). Hawthorne, NY: Walter De Gruyter.

9. Evans, R. (1996). *The human side of school change: Reform, resistance, and the real-life problems of innovation.* San Francisco: Jossey-Bass.

10. Oakes, J., Quartz, K. H., Ryan, S., & Lipton, M. (1999). *Becoming good American schools: The struggle for civic virtue in education reform.* San Francisco: Jossey-Bass.

11. National Association of Secondary School Principals on Middle Level Education. (1985). *An agenda for excellence at the middle level.* Reston, VA: Author.

12. MacIver, D. J., & Epstein, J. (1991). Responsive practices in the middle grades: Teacher teams, advisory groups, remedial instruction, and school transition programs. *American Journal of Education, 99,* 587–622.

13. Galassi, J. P., Gulledge, S. A., & Cox, N. D. (1997). Middle school advisories: Retrospect and prospect. *Review of Educational Research, 67*(3), 301–338.

14. Meier, D. (1995). *The power of their ideas.* Boston: Beacon Press.

15. Rappaport, N. (1999). An advising program in a large urban high school: The magic match. In A. H. Esman, L. Flaherty, & H. Horowitz (Eds.), *Adolescent psychiatry* (pp. 207–223). London: Analytic Press.

16. Galassi, J. P., Gulledge, S. A., & Cox, N. D. (1998). *Advisory definitions, descriptions, decisions, directions.* Columbus, OH: National Middle School Association.

17. Ayres, L. R. (1994). Middle school advisory programs: Findings from the field. *Middle School Journal, 25*(3), 8–14.

18. Powell, L. (1994). Interpreting social defenses: Family group in an urban setting. In M. Fine (Ed.), *Chartering urban school reform.* New York: Teachers College Press.

19. Masten, A. S. (2001). Ordinary magic: Resilience processes in development. *American Psychologist, 56,* 227–238.

20. McDonald, J. (1997). *Redesigning schools.* San Francisco: Jossey-Bass.

21. Rappaport, N. (2000). Small advising groups: Relationships for success. *High School Magazine, 7,* 45–48.

22. Cole, C. G. (1994). Teachers' attitudes before beginning a teacher advisory program. *Middle School Journal, 25*(5), 3–7.

23. Vandenberg, R. (1999). The permanent importance of the subjective reality of teachers during educational innovation: A concerns-based approach. *American Educational Research Journal, 35,* 879–906.

24. Tremlow, S., Fonagy, P., & Sacco, F. (2001). An innovative psychodynamically influenced approach to reduce school violence. *Journal of the American Academy of Child and Adolescent Psychiatry, 40,* 377–379.

25. Rappaport, N. (2001). Letter to the editor re school violence. *Journal of the American Academy of Child and Adolescent Psychiatry, 40,* 378.

26. Erickson, E. H. (1968). *Identity, youth, and crisis.* New York: Norton.

27. Delpit, L. (1994). *Other people's children: Cultural conflict in the classroom.* New York: New Press.

NANCY RAPPAPORT *is clinical instructor in the Department of Psychiatry, Harvard Medical School, and a child psychiatrist and mental health director of the Teen Health Center at the Cambridge Hospital, Cambridge, Massachusetts.*

Index

Adaptive learning, 60–61

Adolescent population: comparing American and Samoan, 59–60; demographics of, 1; emotional or behavioral disorders of, 21; ethnographic studies of preindustrial, 63; as resource to society, 1

Adolescent turbulence, 59

Adolescent-adult relationships: apprenticeship, 17, 84; asymmetric nature of, 96; comparing teacher-student/mentor-youth, 92–93; members' representation of the, 94; mentoring effectiveness and length of, 16–17; mentoring outcomes tied to, 23–24; Mentoring Relationships Model study on, 33–34, 42–43; psychological/behavioral competence contributions by, 26–28; within school systems, 18; strategies for encouraging, 17–18; structural support/guide function of, 91–92; various types of, 18–19; workplace development of, 65–66. *See also* Mentor-youth relationships; Teacher-student relationships

Adolescents: building self-confidence of, 72–73; implementing relational resources for disadvantaged, 96–101; mentoring effectiveness and age of, 64; mentoring outcome and perception of, 27–28; perception of natural mentors by, 26; psychological/behavioral competence contributions by mentors to, 26–28; school primary prevention efforts for, 98–101; sense of self-worth by, 27; study on resilient, 87–88; teaching career planning to, 73–74; value of work experience to, 64–65; workplace mentoring and

disadvantaged, 83–84. *See also* Competence development

Adopt-A-Student Program, 25

Adult role model: mentor-youth relationship and strong, 23–24; mentors as significant, 24–26. *See also* Significant adults

After-school mentoring programs, 5–6

Apprenticeship programs, 17, 84. *See also* Work experience mentoring

Banking time metaphor, 102

Barry, H., III, 63

Battistich, V., 100, 101

Big Brothers Big Sisters of America: age differences and effectiveness of, 64; duration of relationships in, 25; Mentoring Relationships Model study on, 29–36; nationwide affiliates of, 22; predicting mentors as significant adults in, 41–46; Program Effects Model study on, 36; relationships/significant adult mentors in, 42–43; research interest/study on, 10–11; school-based mentoring programs sponsored by, 110; volunteer year commitment requirement by, 15

Biologically predisposed characteristics, 93–94

Bowlby, J., 94

Boys and Girls Clubs of America, 10, 26

Brady, H. E., 84

Brand, S., 98

Bush, G. W., 5

Career planning, 73–74

Cavell, T., 103

CDP (Child Development Project), 100–101

Back Issue/Subscription Order Form

Copy or detach and send to:

Jossey-Bass, 989 Market Street, San Francisco, CA 94103-1741

Call or fax.

Phone 888-378-2537 6AM-5PM PST; Fax 415-951-8553

Back issues: Please send me the following issues at $28 each
(Important: please include issue's ISBN)

1. YD _____

_____

_____

$ _____ Total for single issues

$ _____ Shipping charges (for single issues *only;* subscriptions are exempt from shipping charges): First item: $5.00. Each additional item: $3.00.

Subscriptions   Please ❑ start   ❑ renew my subscription to *New Directions for Youth Development* at the following rate:

US: ❑ Individual $70   ❑ Institutional $135
Canada: ❑ Individual $70   ❑ Institutional $175
All others: ❑ Individual $94   ❑ Institutional $209

NOTE: Issues are published quarterly. Add appropriate sales tax for your state for single issue orders. No sales tax for U.S. subscriptions.

$ _____ Total single issues and subscriptions (Canadian residents, add GST for subscriptions and single issues)

❑ Payment enclosed (U.S. check or money order only)

❑ VISA, MC, AmEx, Discover Card # _____ Exp. date_____

Signature _____ Day phone _____

❑ Bill me (U.S. institutional orders only. Purchase order required)

Purchase order # _____

Federal Tax ID 135593032   GST 89102-8052

Name _____

Address _____

_____

Phone_____ E-mail _____

For more information about Jossey-Bass, visit our Web site at:
www.josseybass.com   **PRIORITY CODE = ND2**

Other *New Directions* Titles Available from Jossey-Bass

CD89 **Rights and Wrongs: How Children and Young Adults Evaluate the World**
Marta Laupa, Editor
Focuses on the way children and young adults understand and form judgements of right and wrong and examines the ways these judgements are independent yet coordinated. Address the formation of judgements of right and wrong within and across different domains of knowledge as well as interrelations or coordinations across judgements of different types. Presents research on judgements of truth and how children distinguish domains of truth. Examines how children judge moral and mathematical rights and wrongs and coordinate them with concepts of authority. Also discusses children's distinction between what is held to be factually true and morally right as well as how they make judgements about moral worthiness and moral obligation.
ISBN: 0-7879-1256-5

CD85 **Homeless and Working Youth Around the World: Exploring Developmental Issues**
Marcela Raffaeli, Reed W. Larson, Editors
Provides a step toward integrating knowledge of street youth into the domain of developmental research. Takes a geographical approach, presenting studies from four different regions of the world: India, South America, Africa, and North America. Explores issues of stress and resilience, cognitive development, identity formation, gender differences, and the development of self-efficacy under harsh conditions. Offers practical guidelines for doing research with street youth, addressing the methodological challenges and ethical issues. Provides a model for understanding homeless and working street youth that synthesizes concerns across disciplines, including medicine and public health, and brings a human rights perspective to the study of impoverished youth.
ISBN: 0-7879-1252-2

CD84 **The Role of Peer Groups in Adolescent Social Identity: Exploring the Importance of Stability and Change**
Jeffrey A. McLellan, Mary Jo Pugh, Editors
Enhances our knowledge of the adolescent peer world in terms of both interpersonal relationships and social categories. Sheds light on an array of questions about adolescent social life, including: How changeable is peer group influence over time? Do adolescents identify with the crowd to which their peers classify them, or do they identify more closely with higher status crowds? How do adolescents form alternative groups that resist the cultures of the dominant peer group? Does having a sibling or dating partner make a difference in other relationships? Illustrates the crucial role that peer relationships play in identity formation, and demonstrates the importance of viewing the peer world as a dynamic and changeable place.
ISBN: 0-7879-1251-4

CD78 **Romantic Relationships in Adolescence: Developmental Perspectives**
Shmuel Shulman, W. Andrew Collins, Editors
Examines demographic studies of dating patterns and deals little with aspects such as the characteristics or development of adolescent romantic relationships. Offers both innovative research and compelling discussions on adolescent romantic relationships.

CD72 **Creativity From Childhood to Adulthood: The Developmental Issues**
Mark A. Runco, Editor
Offers a comprehensive examination of how creativity develops from childhood through adulthood, exploring a full range of issues from the biological underpinnings of creativity across the life span to the differences between creativity in adults and children. Topics include whether creativity in adults is only different in degree, not in kind, from creativity in children; the effects of puberty on creativity; moving beyond Piaget to accept divergent, chaotic, and creative thought; and more.

NEW DIRECTIONS FOR MENTAL HEALTH SERVICES
H. Richard Lamb, Editor-in-Chief

MHS54 **Neurobiological Disorders in Children and Adolescents**
Enid Peschel, Richard Peschel, Carol W. Howe, James W. Howe, Editors
Summarizes scientific data about neurobiological disorders in children and adolescents and discusses treatment approaches based on these findings—particularly pharmacological treatments. Recommends fundamental changes in our society's institutions—including the medical profession, the insurance industry, the educational system, and the legal system—necessitated by these findings.
ISBN: 1-55542-758-8

MHS64 **Assessing and Treating Victims of Violence**
John Briere, Editor
Deals with the assessment and treatment of post-victimization trauma, including childhood sexual abuse. Outlines immediate impacts of childhood sexual victimization and provides a state-of-the-art assessment. Describes a model treatment program for sexually abused children and provides data-based information on effective treatment approaches. Reviews known longer-term effects of childhood sexual abuse and suggests a theoretical framework for organizing and understanding such sequelae.
ISBN: 0-7879-9991-1

MHS77 **Families Coping With Mental Illness: The Cultural Context**
Harriet P. Lefley, Editor
Offers both a longitudinal and a cross-sectional perspective on involving families in the treatment of adults with severe and persistent psychiatric disorders. This issue views culture in a broad sense—

as a set of shared beliefs, values, behavioral norms, and practices that characterize a particular group of people who share a common identity—and examines the impact of cultural differences on mental health theory and treatment. Offers practice guidelines and suggestions for further research in the area of culturally competent mental health care services.
ISBN: 0-7879-1426-6

MHS86 **Psychiatric Aspects of Violence: Issues in Prevention and Treatment**
Carl C. Bell, Editor
Presents a comprehensive examination of the full range of violence-related issues that mental health practitioners may confront in their practice. Provides guidance on how to assess and manage violent patients, how to predict the risk for violence, and how to treat victims of violence. Reviews both the victim and perpetrator aspects of sexual violence, explores the special issues surrounding family violence, and more.
ISBN: 0-7879-1435-5

Made in the USA